Guide To

Cross-Cultural Communication

W9-CNU-678

Prentice Hall "Guide To" Series
in Business Communication

Guide To

Cross-Cultural Communication

Second Edition

Sana Reynolds
Baruch College,
The City University of New York

Deborah Valentine
Goizueta Business School,
Emory University

Mary Munter
Tuck School of Business,
Dartmouth College
Series Editor

Prentice Hall
Boston   Columbus   Indianapolis   New York   San Francisco
Upper Saddle River   Amsterdam   Cape Town   Dubai
London   Madrid   Milan   Munich   Paris   Montreal
Toronto   Delhi   Mexico City   Sao Paulo   Sydney
Hong Kong   Seoul   Singapore   Taipei   Tokyo

Editorial Director: Sally Yagan
Editor in Chief: Eric Svendsen
Acquisitions Editor: James Heine
Product Development Manager: Ashley Santora
Director of Marketing: Patrice Jones
Marketing Manager: Nikki Jones
Marketing Assistant: Ian Gold
Senior Managing Editor: Judy Leale
Production Manager: Meghan DeMaio
Creative Designer: Jayne Conte
Cover Designer: Bruce Kenselaar
Cover Image: Getty Images, Inc.
Full-Service Project Management/
 Composition: Sudip Sinha/Aptara®, Inc.
Printer/Binder: Edwards Brothers
Cover Printer: Lehigh-Phoenix Color
Text Font: Times

Library of Congress Cataloging-in-Publication Data
Reynolds, Sana.
 Guide to cross-cultural communication / Sana Reynolds, Deborah
Valentine. —2nd ed.
 p. cm.
 Includes bibliographical references.
 ISBN-13: 978-0-13-215741-4
 ISBN-10: 0-13-215741-1
 1. Intercultural communication.   I. Valentine, Deborah   II. Title.
 GN345.6.R49 2010
 303.48'2—dc22

                                                2010000453

10 9 8 7 6 5 4 3 2 1
Prentice Hall
is an imprint of

www.pearsonhighered.com ISBN 13: 978-0-13-215741-4
                          ISBN 10:   0-13-215741-1

Contents

PART I
UNDERSTANDING
CULTURES

CHAPTER I

CHAPTER II

CHAPTER III

CHAPTER IV

PART II
COMMUNICATING
ACROSS CULTURES

CHAPTER V

CHAPTER VI

CHAPTER VII

COMMUNICATING NONVERBALLY 75

CHAPTER VIII

NEGOTIATING: PROCESS, PERSUASION, AND LAW 93

Instructor's Preface

CHANGES TO NEW EDITION

Although we have incorporated revisions throughout the book, we would like to highlight some of the most extensive changes:

- *Technology:* Explores ways that new technology impacts cross-cultural communication
- *Millennial generation:* Presents data on the global impact of the millennial generation
- *Updated examples:* Includes updated intercultural examples
- *Applications:* Provides running descriptions for applications of guidelines
- *Audience:* Targets a world-wide audience
- *Readings and films:* Updates suggested readings and films

In addition, we have updated all of the chapters.

In Part I: Understanding Cultures, we examine what motivates people from different cultures to engage in business transactions.

- *Relationships: Individual or Collective?* Some cultures value the group and harmony over the individual and personal competitiveness, and stress relationships rather than actual transactions. Knowing about these differences can help your students establish successful intercultural partnerships.
- *Social Framework: High Context or Low Context?* Some cultures require explicit, content-rich, direct statements when communicating; others rely on an indirect, implicit, unspoken (but generally understood) and accepted context. Help your students learn where particular cultures fall on the high context/low context continuum and how to tailor their communication to meet cultural needs.
- *Time: Linear, Flexible or Cyclical?* The view of time itself differs vastly among world cultures. In the U.S. business culture, time is defined as a linear and precious commodity to be used, not wasted; other

cultures see time as circular, repetitive, fluid, and subordinate to people and relationships. In this chapter, your students will discover how to recognize these different attitudes toward time and communicate their organization's expectations as they relate to delivery schedules and other time related issues.

- *Power: Hierarchical or Democratic?* Many world cultures view the organization of companies differently from the power-sharing, flat structures of most US businesses. We examine ways to establish effective business presence when communicating across hierarchical and democratic power structures.

In Part II, your students will learn to apply what they've learned about cross-cultural persuasion by discussing how to shape written documents and how to communicate orally with sensitivity to nonverbal elements.

- *Using Language:* Even when everyone in a meeting speaks English, misunderstandings occur because of semantics, differing connotations, idiomatic expressions, industry jargon, and untranslatable slang expressions. This chapter discusses how the major international cultural groups use language differently and how these differences can have a profound impact on your students' bottom line.

- *Writing:* Because miscommunication can be especially potent and long-lasting when written, we provide guidelines for developing sensitive cross-cultural writing skills. This chapter addresses the slippery issues of acceptable formats and tone especially when using current technology.

- *Communicating Nonverbally:* The cultures of the world communicate by more than language. In some cultures, nonverbal communication comprises as much as 85 percent of all communication. In this chapter, your students will learn what constitutes effective eye contact, body language, personal space, and how cultures differ in their use of silence.

- *Negotiating: Process, Persuasion, and Law:* Cultures vary in their interpretation of business agreements and contracts. Some value specific and detailed written contracts; others prefer to conduct business through verbal agreements and view legal contracts with distrust. This chapter provides guidance on how negotiating techniques and legal concepts affect communication and discusses ways to establish credibility.

The book ends with a *Conclusion*, a *Cultural Questionnaire* to develop your students' personal awareness, a *Bibliography* listing the sources that shaped the academic and research backdrop for our discussions, and *Suggested Readings and Films* for your students' continuing growth in effective intercultural communication.

WHY THE BOOK WAS WRITTEN, HOW IT IS UNIQUE

We have taught thousands of MBA students and business profession-als at universities and corporations in the U.S. and abroad—and have been both surprised and dismayed at the lack of awareness of effec-tive intercultural communication. Even among people who have worked abroad there is ignorance and misunderstanding.

However, these busy professionals have found other books on cross-cultural communication too long or academic for their needs. That's why Prentice Hall is publishing this series, the *Prentice Hall "Guide to" Series in Business Communication*—brief, practical, reader-friendly guides for people who communicate in professional contexts.

The 2nd edition of *Guide To Cross-Cultural Communication* maintains the unique style of the first edition—which has received consistently positive feedback from both instructors and students.

- *Short:* The book summarizes key ideas from thousands of pages of text and research. We have omitted bulky examples, cases, footnotes, and exercises.

- *Professional:* This book includes only information that professionals will find useful; unlike other books, it is aimed at professionals.

- *Readable:* We have tried to make the book clear and practical. The format makes it easy to read and to skim. The tone is direct, matter-of-fact, and nontheoretical.

VALUE PACKS

Prentice Hall/Pearson offers "value packs" which would allow you to combine *Guide To Cross-Cultural Communication* with any other book in the "Guide To" series. So, if you would like to teach any of the following topics in more detail, consider adding any of the following books.

- ESL and international students: *Guide for Internationals*
- Report writing: *Guide to Report Writing*
- Presentations: *Guide to Presentations*

- PowerPoint: *Guide to PowerPoint* (for PPt. version 2003) *or Guide to PowerPoint* (for PPt. version 2007) depending on which version your students use.
- Facilitating meetings: *Guide to Meetings*
- Interpersonal/listening skills: *Guide to Interpersonal Communication*

If you are interested, please contact your local Pearson Professional and Career sales rep. If you do not know who your local rep is, visit: www.pearsonhighered.com/educator/replocator

To find out the ISBN number for any of the books, visit: www. pearsonhighered.com/munter

About the Authors

Sana Reynolds, a professor at Baruch College, CUNY, is a communication expert and consultant with over 25 years of extensive multinational experience in the United States and overseas; her expertise in cross-cultural and managerial communication has allowed her to successfully coach executives at more than 50 companies worldwide.

Deborah Valentine teaches cross-cultural business communication as well as business communication for international students at Emory University. She is president of the international Association for Business Communication.

Introduction

A closed mind is like a closed book, just a block of wood.
—CHINESE PROVERB

A s the Chinese proverb suggests, the best tool for understanding culture, especially cross-cultural communication, is an open mind. In this guide, we define communication as sending or receiving information either verbally or nonverbally (as we'll discuss in more detail on the next few pages). Cross-cultural communication refers to communication that occurs between people who have different cultural backgrounds. They may come from different countries or may live and work in the same country but still have different cultural backgrounds.

It's a sad fact that many businesspeople interact with those from other countries or cultures without having a good understanding of the very meaning of culture.

> An international banker with three years' experience working in China was asked to discuss some of the cultural characteristics he had encountered. He answered, "Well, they [the Chinese] tended to be shorter than I am, and their skin was darker." This bright, well-educated man had mistaken ethnicity for culture. Worse, even after receiving an explanation of culture, he discovered that he had observed very little of the Chinese culture in his three years working abroad.

As this example shows, the international banker could have benefited greatly from a short course designed to improve cultural awareness. The goal of this book is to serve as your short course in culture—a course that provides the foundation for cross-cultural communication in the business world.

Our first step toward understanding cross-cultural communication is to arrive at a clear definition of culture. We'll also look at what experts have to say about culture and communication. Finally, we'll review a seven-step strategic communication model that will be useful when you communicate across cultures.

I. UNDERSTANDING CULTURES

When we were children, many of us had the experience of being the new kid on the block. For the first few days, everyone wanted to meet us and play with us, but our good luck would wear off if we failed to pay attention. Those of us who were socially adept soon learned the "rules" of the new neighborhood. We quickly found a champion, a kid who would teach us the sometimes invisible protocol. We learned when to talk and when to keep quiet. We learned whom to talk to and whom to avoid—especially the neighborhood bully. We learned how games were played in the new neighborhood—were marbles played "for keeps"? Were most games played in teams? Did the new group value winning or playing fair?

We learned other social rules such as the proper way to address the mothers and fathers of our new friends. Sometimes we taught our new friends games from our former neighborhood. The new group would often modify the rules of the game to better fit their ideas and even adopt some of the "cool" sayings from our old neighborhood. We never realized that what we were learning and sharing was culture.

Experiencing culture on the job: We experience a similar learning curve in any new job. We show up knowing very little of the corporate culture. We know our job description, and may have read the website, but the politics of the place is another matter.

In this situation, a successful businessperson will align with someone who can reveal the corporate culture, help prevent blunders, and provide information on such questions as—how important are relationships in getting things done? Do teams or individuals handle most projects and clients? Would this organization be classified as on time or laid-back? How direct are the lines of communication upward and downward? Is there a pyramid-shaped hierarchy, or does this organization have a relatively flat structure? Is it easy to get messages to the top of the company, or is it important to send them through the proper corporate channels? Are emails preferred to face-to-face meetings? How formal and direct are the written documents? This process of uncovering corporate culture reveals much that is useful in the study of intercultural communication. All the questions that you might ask in a new job can help clarify the very definition of culture.

Defining culture: In this book, we will differentiate between the popular definitions of culture and the definition that anthropologists, sociologists, and psychologists use. The popular or common definition of culture involves music, theater, and art—the things that enrich our lives. However, these popular definitions do not recognize that music, theater, and art are actually derived from a more basic, yet invisible, structure of life. It is that structure that we will define and clarify, because businesspeople that are well informed in cultural self-knowledge will be better able to understand and communicate in increasingly diverse workplaces. Our working definition of culture involves four elements.

- *Culture is acquired:* We learn culture from our parents and others in our community. As children, we learn not to step on the feet of others and how far from each other we should stand while speaking. We learn when to speak, when to listen, and where to direct our gaze when speaking or listening. Even as we are learning our native language, our mothers, fathers, and elders teach us proper modes of address such as Aunt, Uncle, Mr., and Mrs. We also learn idiomatic expressions and slang. If we grew up in the United States, we were probably taught that it's important to be on time and that everything in life runs by the clock.

  By the time we become adults, our culture has become invisible to us. We only notice that someone has done something "wrong" when they stand too close or fail to use proper modes of address. We notice if someone is not on time, and we criticize those who have never learned the "right" way to address a person of authority. Some of us may criticize a person who grew up in a different culture by calling them "Yankee" or "Redneck," for example. All the while, we have no idea that what we are observing and perhaps criticizing involves the concept of culture.

- *Culture is shared:* Culture does not exist in a vacuum. This leads to the next element in our definition of culture—that it is shared.

Although we rarely take note, we expect people to think and behave in certain ways.

Consider that people raised in the United States favor a cause-and-effect reasoning. "If I do X, then Y will happen." We assume that everyone around the world reasons in the same way and that anyone using a different method of reasoning is illogical.

In the same way, we may assume that someone who is habitually late to work and meetings is somehow deficient. We use labels such as "lazy" to describe a person who has a relaxed sense of time even when that person's output is on par with everyone else.

- *Culture defines core values:* Because we have been taught our culture and share our culture with our group, we tend to form the same core values. Just as a corporate mission statement includes values that the corporation holds dear (such as customer service, quality, or community service), groups of people form opinions about the things that are important to them.

A group sharing a similar culture might agree that family holds preeminent value. Other aspects of thinking and behavior will then flow from that core value of the family. For example, believing in the core value of family might mean that colleagues have a benevolent attitude toward a co-worker who takes time off to attend the birthday of a daughter or son.

Another culture might value respect for hierarchy and, therefore, design social and business structures to reflect that value. Instead of sharing power equally, employees would expect to have a clearly defined leader to guide their work and decision making.

- *Cultures resist change:* Based on these elements of culture—that it is taught, shared, and forms our values—we can proceed to an interesting, albeit rarely discussed, aspect of culture. Although culture can and does change, such change is both slow and gradual. We've all talked about changes in corporate culture—"This place is just not the same anymore. We used to really care about each other, but now we don't even know each others' names." If corporations are microcosms of the larger culture, then the fact that they can change is evidence that the larger culture can and does change. For example, the focus on a return to family values in the U.S. reflects the concern that the culture was changing in a direction that was troubling to many. While a change in corporate culture develops slowly, the core culture may take generations to change. When they do occur, such cultural changes rarely reflect huge shifts in core values.

• *Developing cultural awareness:* In the words of an Afghan, "What you see in yourself is what you see in the world." This tendency to project our own beliefs onto others leads to problems in business. Without training in cultural awareness, we quickly label as "wrong" the behavior of those who do things differently. We fail to realize that people from other cultures who are so important to our future in business may be behaving appropriately based on the culture they were taught.

Just as we appreciated the help we received when we were the new kids on the block, we should also give adults from other cultures a chance. In doing so, not only will they learn about our way of doing things, but we will also learn from them. Cultural understanding will enrich our businesses and our lives.

As you begin to sort through your personal culture, you'll better understand how the characteristics we describe apply to your life. To do so, we recommend that you analyze your own culture by completing the "Cultural Questionnaire" at the end of this book. Doing this both before and after you read each chapter will maximize your growth in cultural awareness.

II. LEARNING FROM THE EXPERTS

One path to effective cross-cultural communication is to review the work of scholars and researchers in the field. We'll take a brief look at the work of Edward Hall, Geert Hofstede, and Mary Munter to see what they have to say about culture and communication.

Edward Hall: In a series of books starting with *The Silent Language,* followed by *The Hidden Dimension, Beyond Culture, The Dance of Life,* and *Understanding Cultural Differences,* anthropologist Edward Hall has contributed a great deal to our understanding of culture. Hall defined culture as a form of communication, governed by hidden rules, that involves both speech and actions. He terms culture, "a vast unexplored region of human behavior that exists outside the range of people's conscious awareness." Culture affects everything—especially the relative importance of tasks and relationships.

• *High and low context:* Hall used the terms "high" and "low context" to describe the communication patterns and preferences of a culture. High-context cultures rely on much understood, rather than explicit information. Low-context cultures, by contrast, encompass less understood information and tend to be more explicit and literal. These concepts are particularly useful in business communication because, among other things, they help us to know when to communicate directly and when to be indirect. We'll discuss the differences between high- and low-context cultures in greater detail in Chapter II.

* *Time orientation:* Hall also coined the terms "monochronic" and "polychronic" time orientation. Monochronic time patterns involve a linear view of time as a commodity to be saved, spent, or wasted. Polychronic time patterns are more circular and relaxed and reflect a view of time flowing around us. Hall and his cadre of researchers recognized that time orientation helped to set a culture's patterns of communication. In this book, Chapter III delves into the mystery of the time orientation of cultures.

Geert Hofstede: Sociologist Geert Hofstede conducted an extensive study of employees in a multinational corporation. In *Culture's Consequences,* Hofstede described four dimensions that provide an extremely useful way of analyzing and understanding cultures.

* *Individualism vs. Collectivism:* Hofstede observed that some cultures emphasize the individual while others emphasize the group. Ask yourself what you were taught and what you prefer. Is your ideal the rugged individual or the member of a team? To what extent do you feel obligated to take care of others in your group? Do you believe that you should make decisions based on what's in it for you or what's in it for the group? We examine in depth the cultural focus on the individual or the collective in Chapter I.

* *Power distance:* Power distance is the degree to which the culture believes that institutional and organizational power should be distributed unequally. Were you taught not to question the actions of authority figures? Or were you instead taught that everyone is equal and that any person should feel free to communicate with another regardless of social rank? We will examine power issues more closely in Chapter IV.

* *Uncertainty avoidance:* Hofstede found that some cultures tend to dislike change and avoid uncertainty while other cultures welcome challenges to the status quo. To discover this dimension of your personal culture, ask yourself what you were taught and what you now believe about change and uncertainty. Do you see the unknown as

stimulating? Do you welcome the new and different? Or do you strongly prefer that things stay the same? If you prefer that things stay the same, have you set up rules and structures that ensure that things will be done in a certain way?

- *Masculinity vs. Femininity:* Since even Hofstede himself eventually came to reject his use of the terms "masculine" and "feminine," we encourage you to overlook his labels and think about the extent to which you value achievement and assertiveness over the nurturing of relationships. Do you value a colleague who focuses on advancement and on the bottom line? Or do you believe the most valuable colleague is someone who mentors staff and nurtures talent in others? We'll discuss relational issues in subsequent chapters.

Mary Munter: Communication expert Mary Munter has constructed a model that helps businesspeople communicate effectively across cultures. In her book, *Guide to Managerial Communication* (also cited in the bibliography), Munter provides a seven-step strategic communication model. We explain her seven steps by providing a running example for implementing the model.

- *Setting communication objectives:* What do you want your audience to do as a result of your communication? Based on your knowledge of the other culture, are your communication objectives possible? Is your time frame realistic considering the culture's time orientation?

  In early September, American small business owner, Tom Rogriquez, planned to import patio fireplaces from Chihuahua. The purpose of his call to the vendor was to collect information about the vendor and set a date to meet with him. Because Tom understood the Mexican culture, he knew that he needed to avoid calling on any of the important holidays scattered throughout the year (for example, November 2, Dia de los Muertos or Day of the Dead). He also did not plan to call between 2 p.m. and 4 p.m. local time because his counterpart would probably be at lunch, the most important meal of the day in many Latin American and Mediterranean countries.

  Tom knew that his vendor would be more willing to meet if Tom's timeframe was flexible. He also knew that importing the fireplaces would probably not be possible for the current winter season. Therefore, he adjusted his communication objective. He would try to meet with the vendor in late September and then seek to import and sell the patio fireplaces for the winter season a year later.

- *Choosing a communication style:* What is the most effective communication style given the context of the other culture? Consider Hofstede's dimensions of culture to understand the culture's attitude toward authority, individual or collective focus, and preference for direct or indirect communication.

  Tom spoke fluent Spanish, so he knew that would help in communicating with the Mexican vendor. However, he also realized that his title would be important to the vendor and, therefore, introduced himself as Director of Operations for Decatur Patio & Gift, Inc. Tom also observed protocol in his communication by speaking off the subject during the first part of the meeting. He asked about the weather and Mexico's prospects in the World Cup. Because he was culturally sensitive, Tom was able to select an appropriate communication style and book the appointment.

- *Assessing and enhancing credibility:* How does the other culture establish and assess credibility? Is your rank important? Do they care about your personal goodwill toward them? Is your expertise or knowledge of the subject a critical factor? Do they value image or attractiveness? Is it important that you share their values and standards? (For a more complete discussion of the elements of credibility, see Chapter VIII.)

  Tom's wife, Julie Rodriguez, was active in the business. However, based on the paternalistic nature of the Mexican culture, the couple agreed that Tom would take the lead in establishing the relationship that would lead to years of future business. Once the account was established, Julie would probably make trips to Mexico to continue the business relationship. They knew that if they were successful, the manufacturer would introduce them to other vendors from whom they could export.

  Tom knew to be courteous and polite in both the initial telephone call and subsequent meeting. He might occasionally use profanity when communicating within the U.S., but he would avoid doing so in Mexico's conservative business culture. Being careful of his speech would show that Tom was respectful of Mexican values.

- *Selecting and motivating your audience:* Who should receive your message? Think about rank and authority when you select your audience. Consider what motivates your audience: fair play, material wealth, the challenge of the task, career advancement, achievement and challenge, self-worth, security, satisfaction, personal relationships, group relationships, or perhaps altruism. What works in your own culture may work against you in a different culture. Ask yourself what your audience knows about you and your subject.

Tom analyzed his audience by thinking about what might motivate his Mexican counterpart. He read about the history and landmarks of Chihuahua so that he could visit them before his meeting. He knew that establishing a personal relationship with the vendor would ensure future success. He also knew that he should show fairness in all his business negotiations and that he could expect fairness in return. Because the Mexican vendor did not know him or his business practices, Tom sent a letter in Spanish and enclosed his company's professionally designed brochure and catalogue by way of an introduction.

- *Setting a message strategy:* Consider whether to write, call, or meet in person. Also think about the structure and message formats that will be most effective. Should you be direct or indirect in your communication? Who should deliver your message? What is the best timing for your message?

  Based on his knowledge that relationships form the framework for business in Mexico, Tom knew that he should meet his vendor personally. Phone calls and emails would be part of the communication plan, but face-to-face meetings would be crucial. Tom planned to be more formal and indirect in his communication style and would allow more time and greater attention to the relationship than in typical U.S. business situations, even when using email.

- *Overcoming language difficulties:* Consider the language you will use in your message. Will you use an interpreter? What difficulties might you encounter because of slang, idiomatic expressions, and jargon?

  Even though Tom learned the Spanish language from his parents and spoke it fluently, he knew that idiomatic expressions could be different in the various states of Mexico. Because of this, he knew to be careful and to ask polite questions if he was unsure of meaning. Tom would also ask for recommendations for well-respected translators, as his knowledge of written Spanish was less than polished, and he would need to build a relationship with the translator as well. Tom also planned to have his business cards printed in both Spanish and English to signal his long-term commitment to the business relationship.

- *Using effective nonverbal behavior:* Avoid simply applying your own culture's nonverbal communication patterns to the other culture. Be aware of the types of nonverbal communication that you presently use. What type of nonverbal communication have you observed in the other culture? Personal and conversational space preferences differ widely among the cultures of the world. Think about your personal bubble, the space around you that feels comfortable when you are conversing with another person. Observe the personal space preferred by the other culture. Also consider what greeting behaviors will be most effective when communicating across cultures?

> Tom had learned from his parents the proper greeting behaviors to use on his initial visit to the vendor in Chihuahua, and he was comfortable with a somewhat closer conversational distance than in the U.S. He would shake hands with each person at the meeting and would greet each one. He would not use first names and would be careful to pronounce names correctly. He would wear a suit and tie as a sign of respect.

> Julie knew that when she accompanied Tom on a business trip, she could expect a handshake and kiss on the cheek. If they planned to bring gifts, they would first ask the translator or consultant for advice to avoid an unforgivable *faux pas* such as red flowers—a sign of witchcraft in Mexico. Tom would maintain his integrity and avoid the temptation to use bribes or other shortcuts to business, knowing that the respect he earns will benefit his business for many years to come.

As our running example shows, implementing Munter's strategic communication model will enable you to communicate strategically both within your corporate culture and across international boundaries.

III. GUIDELINES

- *Learn as much as possible about culture:* Diverse cultures have devised a dazzling variety of values and social systems as they attempted to ensure the survival of their members and answer the existential questions of life. Educate yourself about culture—including your personal culture. As you increase your knowledge, accept that people from various cultures are different- and try to view the differences with delight and wonderment rather than dismay.

- *Communicate strategically:* Use the seven-step strategic model to communicate across cultures. In your everyday interactions at the office, begin to enrich cross-cultural understanding by constantly questioning your assumptions about the behavior of others.

- *Avoid over-reliance on stereotypes:* The statements we make in this book describing other cultures are generalizations supported by both research and experience.

These generalizations are necessary as a first step in recognizing differences and acquiring knowledge.

> Richard Lewis, author of *When Cultures Collide,* writes, "We cannot exist without stereotyping—it gives us points of reference in determining our behavior towards strangers . . . it simplifies complex feelings and attitudes. For intercultural understanding we must learn to manage stereotypes, that is, to maximize and appreciate the positive values we perceive, minimize what we see as conflicting or negative."

Rather than being irritated and condemning another's behavior, our guide will help you view those behaviors from a cultural perspective. Your ability to do this will reflect your commitment to becoming a citizen of the world—a sensitive global communicator. Your gain will be great: you will not only become a more effective businessperson in today's global environment, but your life will also become immeasurably richer.

The frameworks constructed in this chapter will be valuable as you read Chapters I–VIII, which explore cultural variables in greater depth.

Guide To

Cross-Cultural
Communication

CHAPTER I OUTLINE

I. Characteristics of individualist cultures

II. Characteristics of collective cultures

III. Guidelines

CHAPTER I

Relationships: Individual or Collective?

He who runs alone will win the race.

—U.S. PROVERB

Better to be a fool with the crowd than wise by oneself.

—MEXICAN PROVERB

One of the most basic concepts that human beings grapple with is the definition of "self." How do we identify ourselves? Do we see ourselves as independent and autonomous, responsible for our own destinies and accountable for our actions? Do we pride ourselves on being self-reliant, risk-taking, assertive, and direct? Are we motivated by personal goals, achievements, and rewards? Or do we see ourselves as interdependent, relational, part of a larger group, seeking harmonious interaction? Are we motivated by group-oriented goals and content to share prestige, reputation, and rewards with others?

If we view ourselves as independent and self-reliant, if we prize personal recognition and achievement, we probably belong to an individualist culture. If, on the other hand, we see ourselves as interdependent, as part of a larger group, if we value closeness and harmony with others over personal goals, then we probably belong to a collective culture.

In his book, *When Cultures Collide*, Richard Lewis argues that these different self-definitions are often programmed into each one of us from a very early age by our cultures.

> When parents, returning from hospital, carry a baby over the threshold, the first decision has to be made—where to sleep. A Japanese child is invariably put in the same room as the parents, near the mother for the first couple of years. British and American children are often put in a separate room—right away or after a few weeks or months. The inferences for the child's dependence/interdependence and problem-solving abilities are obvious.

Although the individualism/collectivism dynamic provides an extremely useful tool for understanding cultural differences, keep in mind the following caveats:

Cultures are seldom monolithic or completely uniform. Every culture has many subcultures which may influence how individuals define themselves. For example, many African- and Caribbean-Americans live in extended family units and prize collective values.

Ethnic communities may cause value variations. Within each culture, different ethnic communities may display distinctive individual and collective values. For example, Native Americans, Middle-Eastern Americans, first and second generation Asian and Latino-Americans, and Americans of Mediterranean descent often retain group-oriented values, especially those promoting the solidarity of the extended family.

Gender may influence values. Various studies show distinct differences in how men and women adhere to individualist/collective values. Many women in individualist cultures are more relational than men. Women tend to value attachment, connection, and caring; men emphasize separation and self-empowerment.

Generations may cause variance. Research shows that individualistic or collective attitudes may be shaped by birth generation. For example, Veterans or Traditionalists (1900–1944), Baby Boomers (1945–1964), Generation X (1965–1980) and Generation Y or NetGeners (1981–2000) often differ in the values they espouse. This is especially true of NetGeners, the first generation to have grown up completely immersed in the internet—shaped by an information-rich, interdependent, collaborative, and immediately-responsive environment.

I. CHARACTERISTICS OF INDIVIDUALIST CULTURES

If you want something to be done well, do it yourself.

—AMERICAN PROVERB

In North America, most of northern and western Europe, and in countries like Australia and New Zealand, people place great importance on individuality, independence, and self-reliance. Children are taught to be autonomous—to think and speak for themselves, to ask questions in class, to make choices, to assume responsibility for their decisions, and to be accountable for their actions. Core beliefs of people in individualist cultures are discussed below.

The pivotal unit is the individual. The goal in most individualist cultures is to develop responsible citizens capable of assuming accountability for personal problems and issues.

- *Life decisions:* Professional and career choices, selection of marriage partners, decisions about childrearing practices and are normally made by the individual with independence as the life goal.

- *Individual identity:* Individualist cultures value individual over group identity. Therefore, individual rights and needs take precedence over group rights and needs.

- *Breakable contracts:* Many people in individualist cultures view all relationships as contracts that can be broken whenever one party chooses; even family relationships or intimate friendships may be severed if they threaten personal goals.

Space and privacy are important. Because individualist cultures value personal freedom, most of them have a greater physical space and privacy requirement than that seen in collective cultures.

For example, Americans value privacy so greatly that they have made it law—Amendment 4 to the Constitution guarantees all citizens the right to be secure in their persons, houses, papers, and effects against unreasonable search and seizure.

This requirement for privacy can be seen in both business and personal environments.

- *In the home:* Individual bedrooms are considered essential, and privacy is viewed as critical to peaceful family life.

- *In the office:* Private offices confer status. Closed doors signal a desire for privacy; entering without knocking is unacceptable.

- *In crowds:* Crowding is perceived as invasive, and when it is unavoidable—in subways or elevators—strict rules (maintaining a rigid body, avoiding eye contact, facing the exit door) govern personal behavior.

Communication tends to be direct, explicit, and personal.   One of the most powerful ways in which human beings express their individuality is through communication. How you express your thoughts, ideas, opinions, and feelings is what makes you unique.

- *Direct explicit messages:* Because individualist cultures value what is unique or unusual about people, they expect communication to reflect the speaker or writer and appreciate clear, direct, and explicit communication that can be decoded easily.

- *Linear logic:* Most individualist cultures have Western European roots; Western logic emphasizes a linear, cause-and-effect thought pattern.

- *Personal accountability:* Messages are expected to capture personal opinion and express personal accountability. Thus, individuals may "sell" themselves and assert their accomplishments in resumes and interviews and assume responsibility for mistakes.

Business is transactional and competitive.   Results are paramount. It is the deal that counts—and business is commonly transacted by scrutinizing facts (due diligence, credit reports, quarterly earnings) and technical competence (past experience, educational credentials).

- *Measurable results:* The focus of business is on results, and success is measured by quantifying profit, productivity, or market share.

- *Competitiveness:* The belief is that competition ensures results. Transactions can be cancelled and contracts can be broken if results don't meet expectations.

- *Separation of relationships and business contracts:* Businesspeople from individualist cultures tend to separate their professional and personal lives, the business deal from the relationship. The goal is the contract, the transaction, or the sale; the relationship is secondary and superficial, just cordial enough to do business. In fact, personal connections or relationships are often avoided; they are seen as muddying the waters, as interfering with objectivity.

II. CHARACTERISTICS OF COLLECTIVE CULTURES

> Two is better than one; three, better than two;
> and the group is best of all.
>
> —AFGHAN PROVERB

In sharp contrast to individualist cultures, the starting point for most human action and decision in collective cultures is the group. Collectivism is common in Asia, Africa, the Middle East, Central and South America, and the Pacific Islands. Children are taught to listen, to defer to elders, to fit in with the family or clan—the group ensures survival. Proverbs and sayings from collective cultures illustrate this belief: "The nail that stands out will get hammered" (Japan), "The duck that squawks gets shot first" (China), "Behind an able man there are always other able men" (Korea), "The sheep that's separated from the flock is eaten by the wolf" (Turkey), "There is no wisdom without the group" (Mongolia), "When spider webs unite, they can tie up a lion (Africa). Let's examine some of the core beliefs of people in collective cultures.

The pivotal unit is the group. Members of collective cultures see themselves as elements in a closely-knit network with others; they are part of a strong cohesive unit (family, clan, profession, corporation, religion) that protects and supports them throughout their lives in exchange for their loyalty.

- *Group decisions:* The individual consults others before making decisions, relying on the group for a broader perspective, and gives priority to group over individual needs. Focusing on purely individual needs is considered selfish, egotistical, and myopic.
- *Collective values:* The "we" is emphasized over the "I", and group rights and needs dominate. Values cherished by collectivist cultures are harmony, personal dignity or "face," filial piety and respect for elders, equitable distribution of rewards among the group, and fulfillment of the needs of others.

  In the collectivist Indian culture, the Hindi will first give you his or her caste identity, then his or her village name, and finally his or her name. In China, Japan, Korea, and Vietnam, the family name precedes the personal name, signaling the importance of family over personal identity.

  Adapted from Ting-Toomey, *Communicating Across Cultures*

Space and privacy are less important than relationships.
Collective cultures generally need less space than cultures that value
individualism. After all, if the group you are part of is important to
you, you may well want to be physically close to its members.

> The Javanese traditionally lived in small bamboo-walled houses that
> have no interior walls or doors. Except for the bathroom, there are no
> private areas. Several anthropologists theorize that, because the
> Javanese have no physical privacy, they have developed a kind of psy-
> chological privacy in their everyday behaviors and communication.
> They speak softly, conceal their feelings, are emotionally restrained,
> and are indirect in their verbal and nonverbal communication.
>
> Adapted from Neuliep, *Intercultural Communication:*
> *A Contextual Approach*

Tolerance for shared space in collective cultures occurs in both
business and personal environments as follows:

- *In the home:* Many members of collective cultures have homes that
  contain one large living area where members eat, sleep, and interact as
  a group. They often live together in extended family groups, tribes, or
  clans and seem to prize personal space less than members of individualist cultures.

- *In the office:* Private offices are far less common and are normally re-
  served for meetings with clients. Members of collective cultures often
  work together at large tables in an open plan office set-up. They spend
  a great deal of social time with workmates and professional colleagues; in fact, it is often during this social time that new ideas are
  discussed, conflicts are resolved, and decisions are facilitated.

- *In crowds:* The attitude of collective culture members towards crowding is best illustrated by the following example:

  > Business travelers often comment with amazement on how people
  > sit in Chinese airplanes. The plane may be virtually empty, yet
  > most Chinese travelers will sit very close together in a tightly knit
  > group. Invariably, Western travelers will spread themselves out;
  > even people traveling together and conversing during the flight
  > will leave at least one seat between them.

Communication is intuitive, complex, and impressionistic. Explicit
and direct communication is less important in collective cultures.

- *Indirect, ambiguous messages:* Meaning is often implicit, inferred, and
  transmitted "between the lines." When a definite message is required
  (e.g., to solve a problem), it is often subtle—rendered indirectly or

ambiguously. The underlying belief is that communication should not be used merely to deliver content; it should nurture the relationship, maintain harmony, and prevent loss of face (personal identity or dignity) by diffusing personal responsibility.

* *Circuitous logic:* Because reality is considered complex, the logic that is employed is seldom linear or cause-and-effect. Situations or problems are presented holistically, within a larger context. Thus, communicators from collective cultures may seem to favor rambling or metaphorical statements.

    The order in which information is presented in Japanese sentences is different. In English, important information tends to be given first, with less important items tacked on the end. In Japanese, less important items are gotten out of the way first, setting the stage for the important information, which comes at the end. The Japanese hint at what has to be done, and even the hints are softened by using impersonal statements in passive constructions.

Business is relational and collaborative.   Most collective cultures believe that relationships, rather than deals or contracts, facilitate results.

* *Subordination of data:* Although facts are not ignored and extensive information gathering and research are common, this hard data is not considered objective or impersonal because words and arguments are not separate from the person expressing them.

* *Relational interpretation of data:* Collective cultures do not see facts as outside and apart from the relationship. Statistical information and analytical measurement are not as important as trust and loyalty to existing relationships. Logic and reasoning by themselves may not persuade; the context of the relationship gives them meaning and weight.

* *Emphasis on the long term:* The focus is on the relationship, the process, growth over time, and building equity. Decisions are not hurried, as consensus is considered desirable.

    Where relationships are paramount, the consensus of the group is important; after all, the entire group will be involved in maintaining and growing an existing relationship. Thus, the Japanese "ringi-seido" method of obtaining consensus stresses "nemawashi," a word that means carefully shaping the roots of a plant to produce the desired result. The belief is that successful implementation of a decision (the plant) requires buy-in from all members in the group (the roots).

    Adapted from Ting-Toomey, *Communicating Across Cultures*

Key differences between individualist and collective cultures are summarized in the following chart:

DIFFERENCES BETWEEN INDIVIDUALIST AND COLLECTIVE CULTURES	
Individualist Cultures	**Collective Cultures**
Transaction oriented (focus on results)	Relationship oriented (focus on process)
Short-term gains	Long-term growth
Emphasis on content (facts, numbers, ratios, statistics)	Emphasis on context (experience, intuition, the relationship)
Reliance on linear reasoning	Reliance on circular reasoning
Independent	Interdependent
Competitive, decision-driven	Collaborative, consensual
Direct, explicit communication	Indirect, circuitous communication
Personal accountability	Protection of "face"
Private offices	Open office plan
Linear time, impatient	Flexible time, patient

III. GUIDELINES: INDIVIDUALIST OR COLLECTIVE?

Use the following guidelines for the two kinds of cultures:

When conducting business in individualist cultures, remember to.

- *Focus on the transaction:* Emphasize the contract or deal and support your proposal with hard data about short-term gains.

- *Use data and logic:* Appeal to competitiveness and present facts, numbers, statistics, benchmarks, best practices, and comparative analyses. Construct your persuasive argument using linear, cause-and-effect logic.

- *Communicate directly:* Prefer direct, clear, and explicit messages. Remember that silence can cause discomfort and doubt.

- *Value time:* Since businesspeople from individualist cultures tend to view time as a precious commodity, estimate the length of time required for a decision or a task, build in "wriggle room" (consider doubling your estimate), and give a precise date by which an answer will be forthcoming.

When conducting business in collective cultures, remember to.

- *Allow time for relationship building:* Build plenty of time to develop the relationship; remember that trust is critical to business. Emphasize collaboration, mutual benefits, and potential long-term growth.

- *Focus on the context of a business relationship:* Pay strict attention to form, protocol, and etiquette; these are essential to preserve "face"—personal identity and dignity. Provide a historical perspective and share background so that your business partners from collective cultures see linkages and connections.

- *Make decisions consensually, contextually, and for the long term:* Be prepared to allot a liberal amount of time to repeated presentation and discussion of the particulars of a deal.

- *Communicate indirectly:* Use silence to enhance comfort level in face-to-face communication. Remember to enhance harmony, preserve face, and provide context for the message using indirect and personal messages.

- *Avoid direct questions:* Avoid asking questions that call for responses identifying accountability. Members of collective cultures are loath to assign blame and are anxious to protect the personal dignity of all members of their group.

- *Be patient:* Plan to spend double the time you think necessary on trips, meetings, presentations, and Q & A sessions. Collective culture members tend to view time as flexible, experiential, and plentiful.

CHAPTER II OUTLINE

CHAPTER II

Social Framework: High Context or Low Context?

A society grows great when men plant trees under whose shade
they shall never sit.
—GREEK PROVERB

God helps those who help themselves.
—AMERICAN PROVERB

Communication expert Edward Hall developed a way to understand cultures by examining their social frameworks and identifying them as "low context" or "high context." Low-context cultures place less emphasis on the context of a communication (such as implied meaning or nonverbal messages) and rely on explicit verbal messages. In contrast, high-context cultures emphasize the context in which a communication takes place and pay a great deal of attention to implicit, nonverbal messages.

Let's look at "context" as it relates to culture by examining the approach of two commercials that aired on international television as well as the internet. These commercials clearly illustrate the contrast between high- and low-context communication.

Commercial #1: A background song plays, "No matter where you go, I will be with you." A little girl says to her father, "Promise you'll call." The father responds, "I promise." The commercial shows the father jetting off to do business and ends with the father calling home and the child running to the phone saying, "Daddy!" Not until the final few seconds of the commercial is the name of the company (Allianz) shown across the screen.

Commercial #2: A duck is shown in various situations where someone has been hurt on the job. The duck repeatedly squawks the name of the company (AFLAC). The text of the commercial defines supplemental insurance as a product that pays if you are injured and unable to work and usually ends with humor.

Both commercials advertise insurance companies, yet the approach is quite different. In the "high context" Allianz commercial, the implied messages are: (1) The company is reliable just as the father reliably calls his daughter. (2) The company is global in nature. (3) The company insures against risk. The "low context" AFLAC commercial includes the following explicit messages: (1) The name of the company, (2) The name of the specific insurance product being offered, (3) A definition of supplemental insurance.

The direct message is repeated several times, as is the company name. The commercial uses physical and situational humor to maintain our interest in what would otherwise be a very plain, direct message.

The preference for either implicit "reading between the lines" or for explicit and direct information varies among cultures. Asian, Arab, and Mediterranean cultures tend to fall on the "high context" end of the continuum whereas U.S., German, Swiss, and Scandinavian cultures fall on the "low context" end. Even within the larger "culture" of the United States, there are regional variations in communication preferences. Northerners and Midwesterners tend to use more literal and explicit communication whereas those from the South tend to be less explicit and direct. Moving from one region of the U.S. to another can create communication challenges, but also provide opportunities for cross-cultural understanding. Hall's analysis of the social framework for messages within different cultures will be useful in helping you create powerful messages when communicating across cultures.

I. HIGH-CONTEXT CULTURES

In this section, we'll examine nine aspects of the social framework of "high-context" cultures. A person from a high-context culture generally:

Relies on implicit communication: People from high-context cultures have been taught from early childhood to look for implied meaning. They believe that what is implied takes precedence over what is said; they will recognize discrepancies between actual words and intended meaning.

> Although the phrase "to rubber stamp" means agreement in U.S. business, the expression would not translate correctly into Japanese. A Japanese report may indeed bear a stamp, but the placement and orientation of the stamp tells the receiver whether the report is acceptable as is, or whether it needs to be reworked and resubmitted. For a report to be approved, the rubber-stamped symbol must be perfectly aligned and not tilt to the right or left. Such subtle messages are readily noticed by those businesspeople who have been brought up in the high context Japanese culture.

Emphasizes nonverbal communication: Although nonverbal communication (body language, facial expressions, gestures and touching, conversational distance, eye contact, etc.) conveys meaning in every culture, people from high-context cultures rely more heavily on nonverbal communication than people from low-context cultures. The nonverbal communication provides the "context" for the conversation and, therefore, must be carefully observed for effective communication to take place.

Subordinates tasks to relationships: In high-context cultures, children are imbued with reverence for family relationships and friendship, as illustrated by the Ukrainian proverb, "Tell me who your friend is, and I'll tell you who you are." A friendship is a deep commitment developed over many years. Businesspeople brought up in high-context cultures carry over the importance of relationships to their transactions on the job. They may believe that a relative with less experience should be trusted over a stranger with more experience in a given job. They may award business contracts to those with whom they have forged relationships over many years rather than to the company that makes the best presentation or offers the best deal on paper.

Emphasizes collective initiative and decision making: A high-context culture values the collective as the important unit of society as exemplified by the Chinese proverb, "A single bamboo pole does not make a raft." Businesspeople from high-context cultures are taught to arrive at decisions that benefit the group. Advancing one's own agenda should never be the stimulus for action; rather, the group or team should initiate, develop, and carry out projects for the betterment of the company and of society. Self-aggrandizement is not only frowned on, it is also not allowed, and an individual risks losing his or her place in the group by "going it alone."

Views employer/employee relationship as humanistic: As you might suspect, the social framework of a society helps determine the relationship between employer and employee, so high-context cultures tend to view the employer/employee relationship in a humanistic rather than mechanistic way. Because these relationships are so important, high-context cultures see employees as "family" members that work for the good of the group and remain loyal to the company for many years. Job performances may vary widely without the threat of imminent dismissal. In addition, the employer will feel loyal to the employees and make decisions based on their welfare. Because trust is an important element in hiring decisions, family members would be preferred over strangers.

Relies on intuition or trust rather than facts and statistics: People from high-context cultures rely on trust or intuition to guide them in decision making. This trust must be established by forming a relationship with the potential business partner and will only be peripherally influenced by the reams of data that someone from a low-context culture might offer.

Intuition or "gut feeling" is a large part of doing business in high-context cultures. Decisions won't be dictated by a plethora of written and spoken information but will be based on a sense of the context of the message.

> Translator Masato Abe tried to explain the importance of "reading between the lines" to his international colleagues. "In English, items obvious from the situation or context are commonly referred to using a pronoun. In Japanese, pronouns are less often used. Rather, known items are simply deleted from the sentence, resulting in sentences

with no subject, transitive verbs with no direct object, indeed, sentences consisting of verbs alone."

In such a sentence, the speaker or writer relies on the receiver's intuition and their relationship to understand the context of the message.

Prefers indirect style in writing and speaking: Given the emphasis on trust in high-context cultures, you may find that business writing and speaking need more space and time to establish rapport. For example, businesspeople from high-context cultures may begin a letter or email entirely indirectly. Only in the second paragraph will they bring up the main point of the business communication. Similarly, in business presentations, speakers will approach the subject indirectly, opening with attention to greetings and acknowledgments. In some, but not all, high-context cultures, it is considered rude to directly state the accomplishments, wealth, or expertise of the company. Instead, these attributes would be carefully intimated, and the focus would remain on mutual benefits. The relative worthiness of the company will be understated. For example, a company representing 28% of the Chinese computer market began their presentation by saying, "We have some small knowledge of this market."

Favors circular or indirect reasoning: People from high-context cultures will discuss issues from a holistic viewpoint with topics arising in random rather than linear order.

A Puerto Rican manager, Juan Marin, was asked to give a brown-bag luncheon talk at the mortgage company where he worked in Houston. The topic for the series of discussions was cross-cultural communication. As he spoke, Juan drew on the white board to illustrate the difference in the preferred reasoning style of his American co-workers. "You talk from point A to point B." Pedro drew a straight line connecting the two letters.

"In my culture, it is different. We do it like this." At this point, Juan drew circles that overlapped eventually forming the pattern of a flower. His artwork drew lots of laughs and comments and was a revelation for those from low-context cultures who sometimes were impatient with Juan's tendency to talk "around" a subject. Most participants did not realize that preference for circular or indirect reasoning is culturally influenced.

Adheres to the spirit of the law: Businesspeople who grow up in high-context cultures generally rely less on written contracts than their counterparts in low-context cultures. People in high-context cultures assume that it's impossible to anticipate every situation that may arise, and, therefore, would feel that agreements need to be revisited periodically in light of the new circumstances. Their attitude is not that laws were meant to be broken, but rather that laws should make sense given the surrounding events and changing circumstance (i.e., the "context" of the situation).

> After "beating my head against the wall," a frustrated American vendor finally realized that she could save time and money by relying less on legal contracts when dealing with a family-owned agricultural supplier in Venezuela. "I now understand that our agreements are fluid, and I've adjusted to that reality." According to the American vendor, "I had to get to know them and vice-versa. Now, we can do business on a handshake and a letter of agreement. It's actually much easier and less expensive than hiring a lawyer to draw up the papers."

II. LOW-CONTEXT CULTURES

In contrast, this section will describe nine aspects of "low-context" culture. A person from a low-context culture usually:

Relies on explicit (literal) communication: Those from low-context cultures prefer that messages be explicitly stated rather than simply "understood" by the parties involved. The following example illustrates the preference for explicit communication in the U.S. Midwest as opposed to the higher context U.S. Southeast.

> Susan Shofield was district manager for a national wholesale shoe company. After rising quickly through the ranks to become district manager of the Southeast U.S., she was surprised that the company wanted to transfer her to the Midwest. Susan, who had lived all her life in the South, knew that the move would be difficult and expressed her concerns to a customer who owned a chain of children's shoe stores in Alabama.
>
> Tom Womeldorf had lived in Springfield, Illinois, most of his life and talked about the adjustment he and his family had to make when they set up shop in the South. "At first, I was too direct, but I learned by listening to my customers how they expected me to communicate. You're a good listener, so it won't take you long to figure out Midwesterners. The people up there say what they mean and mean what they say."

Emphasizes verbal communication over nonverbal communication: The phrase that Susan Shofield heard in the above example ("Say what you mean and mean what you say") is often repeated to children from low-context cultures as they are growing up. Parents place far less emphasis on communicating indirectly or nonverbally and ask their children to "speak up." By the time they enter business, people from low-context cultures have learned to rely on words to convey exactly what they mean. This preference for verbal communication carries over to the workplace where businesspeople are expected to "spell out" what they mean as clearly and directly as possible.

Separates job tasks from relationships: People from low-context cultures usually prefer to keep their job tasks separated from their relationships. Indeed, relationships are seen as outside the task rather than an integral part of it. Even if a key person on a project leaves the company, another person can easily take his or her place since the business transactions are considered to be between companies and not based on relationships between people.

In a training session on cross-cultural business communication at a multinational corporation in Los Angeles, the participants were asked to draw three circles on a piece of paper. One circle represented their family relationships, the second represented job relationships, and the third represented church and community relationships. Participants were asked to draw the three circles to show the extent to which the three groups of relationships overlapped. Out of 20 participants, 12 drew three distinct circles with no overlap. All 12 were from low-context cultures. The participants whose circles overlapped were all from high-context cultures. Neither group had considered that the way they viewed the separation of or the combining of task and relationship was part of their culture.

Emphasizes individual initiative and decision making: Those whose cultures are lower on the context continuum tend to value individual initiative, decision making, and achievement. As the American proverb states, "Look out for number one." Even when they work in groups, individuals from low-context cultures try to think of ways to distinguish themselves as individuals. In business, a group award is valuable and desired, but an individual award is usually more highly prized. The individual is expected to define and solve problems with little supervision.

A professional coach was working with a mid-level manager at a manufacturing plant in Chicago. The coach was from the Euro-American culture, and the manager was West African. One of the "needs" identified by the professional coach was for the manager to establish his individual accomplishments. "Put your name on all your reports, so they'll know that you took the lead on these projects," advised the coach. The West African manager was very troubled by the instructions. It didn't feel "right" to take credit for work done by his team to which he felt much loyalty. The thinking of the professional coach reflected his low-context culture.

Views employer/employee relationship as mechanistic: In low-context cultures, the view of the employer/employee relationship tends to be more mechanistic. The term originates from the belief that a business can be run like a "well-oiled machine" with replaceable parts (i.e., employees). Indeed, employees tend to view themselves as a marketable commodity and will make decisions to change jobs if they can improve their circumstances. Employers can terminate an employee because of negative performance reviews. Likewise, employees feel justified in leaving a job for a better paying one even when they really like their managers and colleagues. Since trust is not as great a factor in hiring decisions, company policy may prohibit the hiring of relatives or even fraternization and marriage among employees.

> A commercial for a U.S. financial company shows a young man talking to his father about a job change. The young man laments the loss of friendships at his old job. He continues by talking to his father about the opportunities in the new job and the ease with which he has rolled over his retirement plan. In response, his father offers support for his decision to leave the old job for the better opportunity even if it means leaving friends at work. He says, "The new job's great. It's going to be OK."

Relies on facts, statistics, and other details as supporting evidence: People from low-context cultures tend to require facts, statistics, and other reliable data in a business presentation. They trust numbers over intuition ("Numbers never lie," American proverb). They may even trust statistical data in spite of special circumstances that could explain a decline in sales, for example. Their presentations will be heavy with charts, graphs, and quotes from experts in their particular field and will be light on suppositions or intuitive remarks. They will often expect the same level of detailed statistical analysis from others.

Uses direct style in writing and speaking: One hallmark of businesspeople from low-context cultures is directness in their writing and speaking. They prefer to get right to the point of their message. Doing so will help them stay on their time schedule and accomplish the task. Therefore, those from low-context cultures usually state the reason for the call, letter, email, or face-to-face meeting at the beginning and then follow with details if asked. Even lengthy business reports will be prefaced with an executive summary of findings.

Prefers linear reasoning: Businesspeople from low-context cultures usually prefer a straight line of reasoning. For example, they may start with reasons a particular account is unprofitable (causes) and follow to the outcome (effect) that the account should be reorganized. They also expect that those with whom they do business will follow the same linear logic. In fact, many people are surprised to find that there exist other kinds of logic. In low-context cultures, "He used circular reasoning to come to that conclusion," is usually not considered a compliment.

Adheres to the letter of the law: People from low-context cultures rarely do business on just a handshake. Even if they have excellent rapport with a business associate, the deal is not considered final until attorneys have written a document that is agreed to and signed by all the decision makers. Conversely, once the signatures are on the dotted line, the contract is set in stone and will be enforced by the courts when disputes arise.

> Because of their low-context orientation, the Jewish culture values precision when it comes to legal rulings. To prepare for a spaceflight mission, Israeli astronaut Ilan Ramon did more than learn about the experiments he would conduct as a payload specialist on the U.S. space shuttle Columbia. Because he planned to observe the Jewish Sabbath in space, he asked for a ruling from Jewish leaders to determine exactly when he should begin and end his observance of Shabbat, the weekly Jewish Sabbath, which lasts from sundown Fridays to sundown Saturdays.
>
> A group of respected rabbis debated and discussed the question. Before the flight, Colonel Ramon received a ruling that he should observe the Sabbath on Eastern Daylight Time because that was the shuttle's point of departure. In the low-context Jewish culture where adherence to the law is revered, such a decision would never be left to chance.

The chart on the next page summarizes major differences between high- and low-context cultures.

SOCIAL FRAMEWORK: CHARACTERISTICS OF HIGH- AND LOW-CONTEXT CULTURES

High-Context Culture	Low-Context Culture
• Relies on implicit communication	• Relies on explicit communication
• Emphasizes nonverbal communication	• Emphasizes verbal communication
• Subordinates tasks to relationships	• Separates tasks from relationships
• Emphasizes collective initiative and decision making	• Emphasizes individual initiative and decision making
• Views employer/employee relationship as humanistic	• Views employer/employee relationship as mechanistic
• Relies on intuition or trust	• Relies on facts and statistics
• Uses indirect style in writing and speaking	• Uses direct style in writing and speaking
• Prefers circular or indirect reasoning	• Prefers linear reasoning
• Adheres to the spirit of the law	• Adheres to the letter of the law

Adapted from Edward Hall

III. GUIDELINES: HIGH OR LOW CONTEXT

Once you have thought about your customers and colleagues in terms of high or low context, you can find a middle ground for effective business communication. For example, if you are from a low-context culture dealing with someone from a high-context culture, you will flex your communication style to obtain the results you desire from your business communication. Follow the suggestions below as you prepare to write or speak.

When conducting business in a high-context culture:

- Understand that contextual information will be important.
- Be aware of the implied messages that you send and that others send to you.
- Develop relationships before focusing on tasks.
- Expect decision making to be collaborative and collective.
- Understand that the employee/employer relationship is humanistic.
- Expect a reliance on trust or intuition.
- Use indirect style in writing and speaking.
- Expect circular reasoning.
- Accept that contracts may change.

When conducting business in a low-context culture:

- Remember that contextual information may be less important.
- Expect a reliance on explicit and direct verbal communication.
- Accept that tasks are viewed as separate from relationships.
- Expect individual initiative and decision making.
- Understand that the employee/employer relationship is mechanistic.
- Support assertions with facts and statistical evidence.
- Use linear reasoning.
- Expect contracts to be firm.

CHAPTER III OUTLINE

CHAPTER III

Time: Linear, Flexible, or Cyclical?

Never put off to tomorrow what you can do today.
—ENGLISH PROVERB

Wise men are never in a hurry.
—CHINESE PROVERB

A ll human beings share time—live in the present, remember the past, and dream of the future—yet cultures view time differently. For example, the United States and Mexico share the same hemisphere and continent, yet they experience and use time in such a different manner that it often causes intense friction between the two countries. The Swiss and German attitudes to time bear little resemblance to neighboring Italy, Spain, or Portugal. For the British, the future stretches ahead; in Madagascar, because the future is unknowable, it flows into the back of your head from behind.

To illustrate these differences, we will discuss the three most common ways cultures define or measure time: cultures that follow *linear (monochronic)* time perform one major activity at a time; cultures that are *flexible (polychronic)* work on several activities simultaneously; and cultures that view time as *cyclical* (circular, repetitive) allow events to unfold naturally.

27

I. LINEAR TIME

If you want your dreams to come true, don't oversleep.
—YIDDISH PROVERB

People in cultures that have a linear concept of time view time as a precious commodity to be used, not wasted. They prefer to concentrate on one thing at a time and work sequentially within a clock-regulated timeframe; this appears to them to be an efficient, impartial, and precise way of organizing life—especially business. Anglo-Saxon, Germanic, and Scandinavian peoples generally live and work by a linear clock; they measure time in small units, value schedules, and focus on the future.

The importance of schedules: In cultures that define time in a linear fashion, schedules are critical because they permit planning and prevent uncertainty. Since these cultures adhere to a cause-and-effect understanding of events and reality, schedules are considered sacred.

People from linear-time cultures make appointments in small segments (15–30 minutes) and dislike lateness because this disrupts the schedule and impacts all subsequent appointments. They prize punctuality and consider promptness a basic courtesy. These cultures deplore interruptions and expect complete concentration on the task at hand; they perceive total commitment as ultimately saving time and view doing two things at once (taking a telephone call or instant-messaging during a meeting) as being inattentive or even rude.

> Walther Habers worked for many years as a commodities trader in Rotterdam. On a business trip to Milan, he waited almost two hours for his 10 a.m. appointment. When the Italian commodities buyer finally came out to meet him, it was time for lunch. Two hours later, after lunch, the pair walked back to the office for the meeting. By this time, Habers was inwardly furious. He would miss his afternoon appointments. Being well traveled, he understood that time was treated differently in Mediterranean cultures, but this was his first experience "in the thick of it." Although he eventually made the sale, Habers swore he would never again "allow such a waste of time." The buyer from Milan, however, was never aware of any problem and thought the transaction had been a great success.

A focus on the future: People in linear cultures so value time that they study time management to learn to get more done every day—an occupation that's often considered absurd by flexible, multitasking, relationship-oriented cultures and impossible by cyclical cultures. Linear cultures' belief in the future is unshakeable—after all, the future promises greater expertise in controlling time and packing more into each time unit. These cultures also view change positively.

> Rana Rakesh, a native of India, moved to New York to become head of sales with an international computer company. She spoke English and three other languages fluently and was well trained in management and sales. After a few months in her new environment, however, Ms. Rakesh became extremely unhappy. "All these people do is rush about with their schedules in their hands," she complained. Ms. Rakesh's manager was very concerned, but for a different reason. He complained that she took too long on a given task. Indeed, he described her as "scattered" in her approach to the project schedules. His solution was to suggest that Ms. Rakesh sign up for a time management course. Ms. Rakesh's response was to resign.

Measuring time in small units: Linear-time cultures (the United States, Switzerland, Germany, Britain, the Netherlands, Austria, and the Scandinavian countries) measure time in relatively short periods: minutes, hours, and days; plan for the short term; and report earnings and profits in quarters and years.

Example expressions: The languages of linear-time cultures abound in expressions which capture the idea of time as a precious entity: "Time is money. Save time. Don't waste time. Use time wisely. The early bird catches the worm." (United States); "He who hesitates is lost. Strike while the iron is hot. A stitch in time saves nine." (England); "Time is everything." (advertising slogan for Swissair); "Uberpunktlich" (German expression for being on time, literally, over-punctual); "Wasting time is stealing from yourself" (Estonian proverb); "Lose an hour in the morning, chase it all day long" (Yiddish proverb).

II. FLEXIBLE TIME

> Time is the master of those who have no master.
>
> —ARABIAN PROVERB

In contrast to linear cultures, cultures that view time as flexible are reluctant to strictly measure or control it. Southern Europeans, the Mediterranean cultures, and the Central and South American cultures are flexible about time. Interruptions are welcome, multi-tasking or clustering is the rule, and relationships take priority over timetables. Although they observe schedules in deference to their linear business associates, most Italians, Spaniards, Portuguese, Greeks, Arabs, and Latinos ignore the passing of time if it means that conversations or human interactions will be left unfinished.

> The personnel files of many U.S. companies are full of stories about Latino or Caribbean employees missing work to meet family obligations. The notion that business can claim priority over a child's birthday celebration or a brother's visit is treated with incredulity. The prevailing attitude is "I can always get another job, but I only have only one brother."

Emphasis on relationships: For flexible-time cultures, schedules are less important than human feelings. When people and relationships demand attention or require nurturing, time becomes a subjective commodity that can be manipulated or stretched. Meetings will not be rushed or cut short for the sake of an arbitrary schedule. Time is an open-ended resource; communication is not regulated by a clock.

> In a recent *New Yorker* article about Mira Nair, the director of the film *Monsoon Wedding,* critic John Lahr described Nair's ability to multi-task and fuse work with family: "Nair turned the final day of shooting into a sort of extended family outing. In addition to orchestrating cast, crew, and a platoon of extras, she was happily entertaining her son Zohran, Lydia Pilcher and her seven-year-old son, and Taraporevala, visiting from Bombay with her two young children. Far from distracting Nair, the swarming confusion seemed to intensify her concentration. 'Her orientation to relationships is very familial. She doesn't work one task at a time or on a purely one-to-one basis. She creates groups,' remarked her husband."

A focus on the present: People in flexible-time cultures tend to focus on the present rather than the future (linear cultures) or the past (cyclical cultures). It's not that they don't value the past nor believe in the future; it's just that they tend to live very fully in the present.

> Nigerian-American Adofalarin Apata had many friends at the technology development business where he worked in Los Angeles. "Ado keeps us centered in the moment," a colleague commented. "We get so focused on the deadlines, that we sometimes forget to enjoy our work, but Ado reminds us to loosen up and enjoy each other and our work."

A reluctance to measure: Although adept at business, many people in flexible-time cultures find the intricate measurement of time or earnings performed by linear-time cultures tedious and unnecessary. When pressed, they will comply with the business contingencies imposed on them by their linear business associates, but their hearts may not be in these calculations.

Example expressions: The famous "mañana" attitude of the Spanish, the often repeated "In sha'a Allah" (If God wills) of the Arab, the Filipino "bahala na" (accept what comes), the Turkish proverb "What flares up fast extinguishes soon," the Mongolian proverb "Profit always comes with a delay," and the Italian proverb "Since the house is on fire, let us warm ourselves" are utterances that capture the subordination of the clock to human reality.

> An American civil engineer, Sam, learned a lot about time differences during his stay in Saudi Arabia. In the U.S. oil company where he worked, there were many Arab engineers. "I would set time schedules, and they would agree. Then, when the deadlines arrived, invariably, there would be a delay. No one seemed upset about this but me. I confronted several of my colleagues to discuss the problem, but they vigorously denied that time was an issue. They claimed there was no difference in the way they approached these projects and that the projects would be finished on time, 'Allah willing.'"

III. CYCLICAL TIME

With time and patience, the mulberry leaf becomes a silk gown.
—CHINESE PROVERB

Although in fundamentally different ways, both linear-time cultures and flexible, multi-tasking cultures believe they manage and control time. In cyclical-time cultures, however, time manages life, and humans must adjust to time. In these cultures, time is neither viewed as linear nor as event/person related, but as cyclical, circular, and repetitive. The human being does not control time; the cycle of life controls people, and they must live in harmony with nature and subscribe to the cyclical patterns of life. Examples of cyclical-time cultures include many Asian, African, and Native American cultures.

> Tatsuo Yoshida, former director of the Industrial Bank of Japan, vividly captured the disparities between linear time and cyclical time. In an interview reported in *Nation's Business,* Yoshida-san stated that the Western business culture is like hunting, whereas in Japan, business is conducted more like rice farming. Japanese business focuses on the long -term; American businesses aim for immediate returns on investment.

Understanding connections: Cultures that subscribe to cyclical time seek to understand linkages and connections. Links show the wholeness of life and allow contrasts or contradictions to exist. Cyclical cultures believe that logic is not linear (cause-and-effect) nor people-driven but captures the unity of human experience with the whole of life, nature, and existence.

> The Masai, a nomadic culture of Kenya, do not compartmentalize time into minutes and hours but instead schedule time by the rising and setting sun and the feeding of their cattle. The typical Masai day begins just before sunrise, when the cattle go to the river to drink. This period is called "the red blood period" because of the color of the sunrise. The afternoon is "when the shadows lower themselves." The evening begins when "the cattle return from the river." Seasons and months are determined by rainfall—a particular month lasts as long as the rains continue and a new month doesn't begin until the rains have ceased.
>
> Adapted from Neuliep, *Intercultural Communication:*
> *A Contextual Approach*

Making decisions: In cultures that subscribe to a cyclical view of time, business decisions are reached in a very different way. Decisions are neither made quickly nor in isolation, purely on their present merits with scant reference to the past; decisions have a contextual background and are made long term. Unlike linear cultures which see time passing without decision or action as "wasted," cyclical cultures see time coming around in a circle, again and again. The same opportunities will recur or re-present themselves when people are that many days, weeks, or months older and wiser. Many cyclical-time cultures will not tackle problems or make decisions immediately in a structured, sequential manner; they will circle round them for a suitable period of reflection, contemplating the possible links between facts and relationships, before committing themselves.

> In his position as Vice President of sales in a U.S. software support company, Tom Batton was eager to offer a promotion to a promising new hire, Ying Zi. Once senior management accepted his proposal, he met with Ying to describe the responsibilities of the new position. Tom had anticipated that Ying would be flattered and excited about the new job, but instead she said nothing for many long moments and then asked if she could consider the proposal for two weeks. Flabbergasted, Tom said, "No, I need your decision on my desk within 24 hours."
>
> Ying discussed the situation with her mentor at the company. "How can he expect me to make such an important decision in only one day? I will need time to contemplate this offer. In fact, I really wanted to ask for several months to make my decision, but I was aware that would not be possible." The mentor intervened to ask Tom for more time and to encourage Ying to speed her decision since in the U.S. "Time is money."

Forging relationships: Although people from cyclical-time cultures may have a keen sense of the value of time and respect punctuality, this is dictated by politeness or by form and will have little impact on the actual speed with which business is done. A liberal amount of time will be allotted to the repeated consideration of the details of a transaction and to the careful nurturing of personal relationships. And it is the forging of a relationship that is all-important; business is facilitated by a degree of closeness, a sense of common trust, connection, and linkage that informs both the present deal and future transactions.

Focusing on the past: People in cyclical cultures pay a great deal of attention to the past because they believe they can find many links and connections there. Since their focus is on the unity of human experience with the whole of life, planning is very long term indeed (decades), and earnings per share or per quarter are far less important than the building of equity.

> A management consultant on assignment in Hong Kong reported that the concept of planning for the short term was quite foreign to the HK business owners she worked with. "I continually heard business plans prefaced with descriptions of 'my company in the time of my grandchildren.'"

Example expressions: Expressions that capture this cyclical view of time proliferate in Sino-Tibetan languages: the Chinese use "wa" (harmony), "han xu" (implicit communication), "gan qing" (a multidimensional set of relational emotions), and "ting" (to listen with ears, eyes, and heart); the Koreans value "nunchi" (an affective sense by which they can detect when others are pleased).

Key differences in the way cultures view time are summarized in the chart on the facing page.

CULTURAL VIEWS OF TIME			
	Linear	**Flexible**	**Circular**
Attitude toward time	An entity to be saved, spent, or wasted	Fluid and flexible	Circular and repetitive
Task completion	Completes tasks sequentially	Works on multiple tasks simultaneously	Completes tasks over a long period of contemplation and reflection
Task vs. relationships	Strives to complete tasks within a certain time frame	Nurtures the relationships represented by the tasks	Values the long term in tasks and relationships
Work vs. relationships	Separates work from family and social life	Views work, family, and social life as one	Focuses on the long term in tasks and relationships
Locus of control	Controls time by maintaining a rigid appointment schedule	Reacts as the day's events evolve	Believes that life controls time
Focuses on	The future	The present	The past

IV. GUIDELINES: ATTITUDES TOWARD TIME

Despite the impact of new media technologies on our view of time (email, blogs, texting, twittering, tweeting, and streaming videos), these culturally influenced differences in time orientation continue to be critical because they can color the way people view each other. For example, a manager who tells time linearly and focuses on the future may view her business partner from a cyclical, past-oriented culture as too tied to tradition to move with the times. In turn, a businessperson from a flexible-time culture may see her linear-time business associate as a slave to efficiency and materialism, incapable of enjoying life, appreciating culture, or developing a real relationship.

Where does that leave us? How do we conduct business with people who measure time differently?

Because business demands a certain synchronization of schedules and goals, most cultures will allow the linear-oriented concept of time to dominate to some extent. But your understanding that their underlying beliefs about the "best" use of time are radically different will allow you to communicate with more sensitivity. The following guidelines should help.

When conducting business in linear cultures:

- *Respect schedules.* Be prompt for business appointments and understand that you will have a brief period to make your point. Most businesspeople from linear cultures schedule their days in 15–30 minute increments.

- *Focus on the meeting.* Don't answer your cell phone or perform any other task. Remember that people from linear cultures expect your full attention and interpret multi-tasking as disrespectful.

- *Target the short term.* Linear businesspeople expect data and analysis that address immediate or near-future gains and issues.

When conducting business in flexible cultures:

- *Depersonalize the issue.* Don't interpret lateness as disrespect to you or lack of commitment to the business goal. Recognize that business objectives may take the back seat to familial or relational concerns.

- *Provide a wider window of time for the appointment.* Building flexibility into your schedule will go a long way to reducing common irritation—"I'll wait in your office from 11:00 to 11:30" or "I'll be in my hotel room from 9:00 to 10:00 and will wait for your call."

- *Clarify expectations.* It's becoming increasingly acceptable to ask: "Is that 12:00 American time or Mexican time?" to determine the actual intended start time of a meeting or social event.

- *Avoid strict deadlines whenever possible by adding some wiggle room.* State—"The delivery date is between Wednesday and Friday" or "The contract needs to be finalized by the second quarter of 2003."

When conducting business in cyclical cultures:

- *Be punctual.* Be on time for your appointment, understanding that lateness is a violation of form and will be interpreted as impolite and disrespectful.

- *Maximize "face" time.* Allow time to build a relationship and remember that face-to-face interaction is preferable to electronic or written communication.

- *Be patient.* Understand that cyclical cultures process information slowly and should not be hurried. Their logic may not be yours; they look for connections and pay a great deal of attention to atmosphere and intuition.

- *Check comfort level.* Remember that because many cyclical cultures communicate indirectly, nonverbal behavior may provide much-needed information. Use culturally-sensitive perception statements or questions to check comfort level: "From your tired facial expression, I can see that you need me to slow down. Am I reading you correctly?"

CHAPTER IV OUTLINE

I. Hierarchical cultures

II. Democratic cultures

III. Signs and symbols of power

IV. Guidelines

CHAPTER IV

Power: Hierarchical or Democratic?

Equality is only found in the graveyard.

—GERMAN PROVERB

A good leader is like rain, calming the ocean.

—HAWAIIAN PROVERB

The way we view power varies widely across cultures, and power affects communication in myriad ways. One approach to thinking about power is to consider what researcher Geert Hofstede described as "power distance." Hofstede defined "power distance" as the communication distance between the most powerful and the least powerful people in a society.

In "high power distance" cultures, communication tends to be restricted and emanates from the top of the hierarchy. Indeed, high power distance may indicate that communication is a carefully guarded tool for protecting and maintaining the hierarchy. Communication between individuals and corporations in "high power distance" cultures will often occur through a well-placed and knowledgeable mediator.

In "low power distance" cultures, the distance between the more powerful and the less powerful is smaller and communication flows up as well as down in the hierarchy.

Hofstede's theory can shed light on the control and flow of information. The chart below summarizes the results of Hofstede's study of employees in a multinational corporation.

HIGH TO LOW POWER DISTANCE COUNTRIES (100 Point Scale) Higher point value indicates high power distance. Lower point value indicates low power distance.		
Philippines (94)	Mexico (81)	Venezuela (81)
India (77)	Singapore (74)	Brazil (69)
Hong Kong (68)	France (68)	Columbia (67)
Turkey (66)	Belgium (65)	Peru (64)
Thailand (64)	Chile (63)	Portugal (63)
Greece (60)	Iran (58)	Taiwan (58)
Spain (57)	Pakistan (55)	Japan (54)
Italy (50)	South Africa (49)	Argentina (49)
United States (40)	Canada (39)	Netherlands (38)
Australia (36)	Germany (35)	Great Britain (35)
Switzerland (34)	Finland (33)	Norway (31)
Sweden (31)	Ireland (28)	New Zealand (22)
Denmark (18)	Israel (13)	Austria (11)

Even though Hofstede's country results may need to be revisited, his concept is nonetheless compelling. We are all aware of organizations with high and low power distances—whether they be military, governmental, corporate, regional, or country-specific—and that awareness can help us communicate more effectively.

"High power distance" cultures tend to have strict hierarchical power structures; "low power distance" cultures tend to have flatter or more democratic social structures. We'll examine hierarchical and democratic cultures in the next two sections of this chapter.

I. HIERARCHICAL CULTURES

One way to ensure power within an organization is through a well-structured hierarchy. One of the many lessons that U.S. businesspeople learn in communicating across cultures is that the relatively democratic organizational patterns of most American businesses can create challenges when communicating with countries that traditionally observe a more hierarchical organizational structure.

> An American group representing every segment of an agriculture-based industry traveled to four Asian countries to promote trade. The group included growers, manufacturers, processors, and researchers. A cross-cultural communication challenge occurred during the group's first stop in Kyoto, Japan. The Japanese businessmen and government representatives who met the group at the designated conference room politely inquired, "Who is your leader?" The first reaction of the Americans was laughter. They were all leaders in their segments of the industry and would not have presumed to designate any one person over another.
>
> After concluding a less-than-successful Kyoto meeting, the Americans sought help from their embassy at their next stop, Tokyo. There they learned that the Japanese prefer a strict hierarchy in their organizations and that promotion in Japanese government and businesses is usually based on seniority. The group held a quick meeting to decide how to make their next meeting more successful. Everyone looked up to Gene, a well-respected senior researcher.
>
> At the second meeting, when the Japanese politely inquired, "Who is your leader?" the Americans were ready. The Japanese placed Gene at the seat of honor and served him tea before the others. The meeting was successful, and the Americans and the Japanese formed a relationship that led to an agreement by Japan to import 20,000 metric tons of the U.S. commodity.

In the above example, the Americans were unprepared for the necessity of naming a leader for their group. They had expected the Japanese culture to be collectivist and to reach business decisions by consensus over time; they did not anticipate the need for a clearly defined hierarchy.

Why do some cultures prefer hierarchical organizational structures and others do not? One answer lies in the comfort these structures provide—a concept that helps people within a culture avoid uncertainty. Three elements of Confucian thought help explain the Asian culture's preference for a clearly defined hierarchy.

Harmony: Eastern cultures believe in maintaining a surface social harmony called "wa" (formed from the Chinese character for "peace") or "chowa" (formed from the Japanese characters meaning "a neat arrangement" and "peace"). In his book, *Confucius Lives Next Door,* T.R. Reid calls "wa" the "preeminent social value" and "the highest goal of human endeavor." People from Asian cultures believe that knowing who is in charge is a good way to preserve harmony; therefore, business situations with a defined hierarchy are more comfortable for them.

Face: A clear and structured hierarchy also helps preserve face and maintain respect. Face can be loosely defined as personal dignity. To those from Confucian cultures, losing face can be devastating and involves not only embarrassment but profound shame. Because of their collectivist culture, one person's loss of face brings shame on the entire group. Knowing the lines of power and authority by maintaining a clear hierarchy helps businesspeople maintain face. If you wish to communicate effectively across cultures, you must be aware of the importance of face.

> In her first meeting as team leader for a North American software company, Jessica Shultz counted on several people in her team to be supportive. She had carefully built relationships over the years so, that when she became a team leader, she could rely on others for allegiance and cooperation.
>
> At this meeting, Jessica asked a very direct question of a Korean American, Linn Park, an expert in product development pricing. Linn, however, didn't have the numbers readily available. Jessica stated that the lack of numbers was not a problem and that Linn could get back to the team with the data later in the week.
>
> Linn, humiliated by the directness of Jessica's question and her inability to properly answer the financial question, immediately requested a transfer to a different division. Jessica had failed to understand the concept of face in maintaining good relationships with those influenced by the Asian culture. She repeatedly met with Linn and over time was able to rebuild a strong relationship.

Paternalism: Confucian beliefs strictly define the duties and responsibilities of relationships that are inherently unequal, such as that of manager and line worker. Such cultures are more comfortable with a clear hierarchy in business, government, religion, and even family life. Those who are more powerful in these unequal relationships are expected to exercise their power in a benevolent fashion. For example, the director of a company has power over subordinates, but his directives should benefit the workers for whom he is responsible, and his workers should respect the hierarchy and welcome the protection it affords.

Eastern cultures aren't the only ones that are paternalistic. Many Latino and Mediterranean cultures as well as most Arab cultures of Africa and the Middle East tend to prefer well-defined power structures in which the person at the top bears responsibility for those who are less powerful. These cultures stand in stark contrast to the United States, Northern Europe, Australia, and New Zealand, where more flat or democratic hierarchies are preferred.

II. DEMOCRATIC CULTURES

Hierarchies tend to be less rigid in the U.S., Northern Europe, Australia, and New Zealand. In Western businesses, hierarchical structures do not necessarily define power. Rather, the hierarchy is used to define job tasks. For example, an organizational chart will show who reports to whom, and job descriptions will ensure that the appropriate people in the corporation complete tasks and solve problems. However, most people in Western cultures think of themselves as equal to everyone else. Because their organizational structure is less hierarchical, Western cultures tend to allow a free flow of information. We'll look at three aspects of democratic cultures: equality, information flow, and responsibility.

Equality: Former CEO of Southwest Airlines, Colleen Barrett, stated, "I think we have tried very hard at Southwest not to talk in terms of rank or jurisdiction." No matter what their job descriptions, workers in more democratic cultures may consider themselves as colleagues with differing levels of responsibility. A good example of a flat organizational structure can be observed in most American MBA classrooms where the professor performs the job of group facilitator and is approachable by the students.

> In his native India, Dr. Vinay Patel was a well-respected professor of business. His style of teaching and classroom organization was typically hierarchical. His Indian graduate students were respectful and his undergraduates worshipful. In class, students didn't challenge him or each other unless specifically invited to do so. When Dr. Patel accepted a two-year position as visiting professor at a well-respected university in Chicago, he brought his assumptions about hierarchy to class with him.
>
> After two months in the U.S., Dr. Patel's assessment of American MBA students surprised his Dean. "These students do not show proper respect for the professor. They love to hear themselves talk and argue openly in class. One would almost believe that they think their knowledge is equal to that of the teacher."
>
> The Dean realized that she would need to do a better job of explaining the flat hierarchical structure of the American classroom to Dr. Patel. She invited him to sit in classrooms taught by other professors so that he could see that the students' behavior was not directed at him and was not meant as a sign of disrespect. By learning to

recognize his cultural assumptions about hierarchy, Dr. Patel made a successful transition to the more democratic culture of the American classroom.

Information flow: In Western cultures such as the United States, Northern Europe, Australia, and New Zealand, communication tends to flow both upward and downward, rather than from the top-down as it would in more hierarchical cultures. In the United States, Microsoft and other high-tech companies have traditionally enjoyed a notable absence of rank and free flow of information. In such corporations, anyone can approach anyone else with ideas, suggestions, or complaints. For example, Microsoft's founder and former CEO, Bill Gates, personally answered hundreds of emails each week from people in his company who had ideas or issues.

Responsibility: In a democratic or flat organizational structure, everyone may share information, but that begs the question of control of the unlimited information flow.

> A corporation in the Southeast was sued for slandering a former executive. Employees were instructed not to talk to media representatives until the suit was settled. When email archives were subpoenaed, however, it became clear that communication about the lawsuit had occurred despite the directive.

Additional questions about responsibility in flat power structures include: "Who should report company goals and profits to shareholders?" and "Who is responsible for reporting abuses?" Deciding who should initiate communication that will benefit the corporation and shareholders can be a tricky issue in cultures where everyone is equal. Corporations employ public relations and corporate communication teams to help control the unrestricted flow of information. Most major universities provide management communication courses to teach clear and responsible communication within corporations and with external audiences.

III. SIGNS AND SYMBOLS OF POWER

Now that we've discussed hierarchical and democratic cultures, let's look at the many ways that societies provide signs and symbols of power. Be wary of hasty assumptions about other cultures because you will invariably be surprised when you are the foreigner.

> A U.S. team from an international paper company arrived in Japan. They had been instructed to observe the dynamics of the other players and to get a "feel" for the person who would ultimately be the decision maker. When they traveled in two vehicles to the company site, one of the U.S. team remarked, "Well, Kazuto Saeki is driving. He must be the team leader." Their translator seemed amused. When asked, he explained that the driver of the other vehicle was likely a junior member of the Japanese team. The most important member would be sitting in the back seat because "that is the place of greatest safety."

Education and profession: A person's education and choice of profession may indicate power. In France, for example, government officials are respected because of their education in the most demanding and prestigious institutions. In the United States, any profession that earns great wealth is more highly respected than professions that may serve the public but earn less. Advanced education in the United States does not necessarily mean a higher-paying job, as many PhD's in Liberal Arts can attest. Unlike public attitudes in the American culture, Asian cultures hold teachers in very high esteem.

Also unlike the United States, those in the professions in Great Britain (government official, attorney, physician) are more respected than those who pursue business (entrepreneurs and other business owners). In fact, the well-educated upper class in Britain has historically been expected to avoid going into business. Even today, there is an unspoken rule among the British that it is poor form to discuss salaries and bonuses.

Family connections: In some cultures, a person's family status and connections may be just as important as education or hard work. For example, in many Latin American and Mediterranean cultures, family connections can open the door for employment. It is only in very individualistic countries such as Australia or the United States that nepotism is abhorred and even outlawed and married couples are forbidden to work in the same division. In fact, in business proposals, family relationships are sometimes hidden. The desire is to "go it alone" rather than relying on support from a family name.

> Joe Barruck, an Australian venture capitalist, hosted a series of presentations by hopeful representatives from Bangladesh, Lebanon, and Brazil. Later, he complained to his associates, "What the heck were they thinking? Every presenter spent way too much time explaining the relationships of the team members and not enough time on the proposal itself. I could care less who their family is; I want to see the project."

Age: Advertisers know that youth is revered in the United States. Older people are given little respect in marketing and in business and are often depicted as bumbling, forgetful, or simply out of date. Unlike the youth-oriented American culture, advanced age is symbolic of wisdom in many cultures around the world. In fact, the advanced age of a person earns special respect in many countries, and this respect carries over to attitudes in the workplace. In Asian cultures, the teachings of Confucius specifically address the relationships between older and younger members of society and instruct young people to respect and obey their elders.

Gender: Gender can indicate relative power in many countries. In cultures where women's contributions are not highly valued, one can assume that the men hold power and authority over the women in a mixed group. Indeed, in conservative Arab cultures, a businessperson would be surprised to see a group consisting of both men and women because the genders are forbidden to mingle.

Language, dialect, and accent: In many cultures, language demonstrates power. A direct or indirect mode of address can indicate position in the hierarchy as those with less power may use indirect styles to address those who are more powerful. Studies have shown that women tend to communicate indirectly in all cultures, often framing statements and observations as questions or suggestions.

In addition, in countries such as England, Argentina, or Germany, a person's dialect or accent can reflect who is more powerful in a communication exchange. Accent can indicate whether a businessperson is from an urban or rural background, and this difference can identify the relative power of the speaker.

Attire: Although a formal business suit once represented power in the U.S. business cultures, in recent years, even very senior businesspeople have chosen to dress more casually in everyday office situations and wear business attire for meetings with external clients and customers. Formal attire is still the norm for business in many cultures, however— "A smart coat is a good letter of introduction" (Dutch proverb). Since formal cultures expect powerful people to wear formal business attire, they may misinterpret casual dress as a lack of respect, and that can complicate the communication exchange.

> A Korean electronic media firm reportedly backed away from negotiations with a major Hollywood production company because of a difference in formality of attire. The Hollywood representatives wore blue jeans while the Koreans wore suits.
>
> Even though the meeting had been billed as "informal," the Koreans believed they were showing their counterparts respect by wearing Western style business suits. The difference in the way the two cultures viewed the importance of attire created a communication barrier that proved impossible to overcome.

Those who would be successful in communicating across cultures will take the time to ask about the proper attire for a particular business meeting or function. For example, women who wish to do business in conservative Arab countries should wear long-sleeved blouses and long skirts. Doing otherwise would indicate a lack of respect for the beliefs of their counterparts and would form a barrier to communication.

Titles and greetings: The use of titles can indicate hierarchy in many cultures. Greeting behaviors can also indicate who is more powerful. In Japan, the businessperson who is lower in rank must perform the lower bow. In India, the "namaste" (hands together in a prayer position at chest level and a nod of the head) can indicate respect or acknowledgement of a higher authority. In military cultures, the soldier of lower rank salutes first and holds the salute until the higher-ranking officer answers it. Even the American tradition of a firm handshake can be misinterpreted if used incorrectly in another country. An American meeting a Pakistani group would be expected to shake hands with each individual at both the beginning and ending of the meeting, even if 20 or more people are present. Businesspeople within a culture sometimes know shortcuts such as shaking hands with the higher ranking members of the group and then placing the hands over the heart to indicate a symbolic handshake with the rest.

In the democratic structure of the U.S., a person's title is sometimes ignored. Even when businesspeople barely know each other, they tend to use first names. Such informality helps convey the flat hierarchical or democratic structure valued in the U.S. culture. This is not always the case in England where a newly hired chief financial officer of a London bank was somewhat startled the first day at work when an administrative assistant addressed him as "Steve."

In more hierarchical cultures, using first names can inhibit effective communication. For example, in Germany, France, or Mexico, speakers should always use titles such as Mr. or Dr.

> An American director of an agricultural research foundation flew to Munich to give a review of his foundation's work. He had been instructed to be formal in his mode of addressing those who attended his talk. The evening before his speech, the American had a wonderful dinner with several key people and established excellent rapport with several of the researchers and scientists.
>
> The next day when he gave his formal talk, he sometimes forgot to address those he had met by their titles and last names. Fortunately, the director had an excellent interpreter who understood the correct use of titles. When the director referred to "Wolfgang," he could hear the interpreter translating the reference as "Herr Doctor Schmidt."

Office arrangements: It's easy to recognize the president of a U.S. company where there's a strong hierarchy. You would look for the spacious window office with exquisite leather furniture and fine art. In other countries, a desk in a central location with many others arranged before it would show who is in charge.

> In the U.S. movie *Rising Sun,* one of the junior members of a large Japanese company tampers with evidence in a murder case in order to protect a U.S. senator. At the end of the movie, his superiors discover his deceit, and he is taken away for a return trip to his native land. An American investigator who had lived many years in Japan remarked, "He will be given a window office." The meaning is clear to those who understand Japanese symbols of power. In their collectivist culture, to be in an office off the main floor is to be shoved to the side, to be ignored, and in this case, to be shamed.

To communicate effectively across cultures, businesspeople must observe and recognize all the various signs and symbols of power.

IV. GUIDELINES: ATTITUDES TOWARD POWER

As the African proverb states, "No one is without knowledge except the one who asks no questions." Use the following questions when preparing to communicate across cultures. Answers to these questions will reveal information about power and hierarchy.

- *Power distance:* What is the power distance of the corporation? To what extent is it distributed unevenly within the organization?

- *Flow of information:* How does communication tend to flow within the organization? Cultures that have well-defined hierarchies tend to communicate top-down. Cultures that have flat hierarchical structures tend to communicate both upward and downward.

- *Paternalism and social responsibility:* How strong is the responsibility for those in power to make decisions that are in the best interests of lower level employees? In cultures that are hierarchical, those at the top of the hierarchy are normally responsible for making decisions that will not harm those at the bottom.

- *Titles and greeting:* What expectations do those in power have for greeting and nonverbal behaviors? Use of titles, the use of mediators for communication upward in the hierarchy, bowing, and other greeting behaviors should be carefully considered when preparing to communicate.

- *Age and gender:* Are older people in the company respected? Are women and minorities given positions of leadership in the company?

- *Education and profession:* Does the corporation respect educational background? Will your profession be an asset or a liability?

- *Family affiliation:* Would employees rather work with people whose family backgrounds they know, or will family affiliations be a liability?

Once you've asked these questions to help you understand your communication audience, we suggest the following:

- *Choose a leader.* If you are from a more democratic or flat-structured culture where power distance is low, designate a person of authority to be the spokesperson for your business transactions when communicating with a more hierarchical "high power distance" corporation. This authority figure should take the lead in asking questions and in answering or directing others to answer questions in business transactions. In cultures with a "high power distance," it may be necessary to communicate through a mediator who has special expertise, family connections, and knowledge of local customs.

- *Find a translator familiar with the culture.* Because the translator plays a vital role in the success of your business venture, make sure you select someone with the proper accent and credentials such as matriculation from a respected university. Ask for recommendations from other companies who have worked with the translator. Acquaint the translator with your objectives and ask the translator to identify persons of authority before the meeting begins.

- *Learn protocol.* Learn proper modes of respect. Hire a consultant who can assist you with: (1) titles and proper pronunciation of names, (2) proper attire, (3) greeting protocols—shaking hands, bowing, etc., (4) personal vs. formal ways of addressing individuals, (5) use of ritual—sitting or standing, business card exchange, and other ceremonies.

CHAPTER V OUTLINE

CHAPTER V

Using Language

He who uses words well is at home anywhere.
—Dutch proverb

If we are to successfully communicate across cultures, we must recognize the power of language. Think of how language can be charged with feeling, how it can galvanize and cause upheaval:

Give me liberty or give me death!
Deutschland über alles!
Liberté, égalité, fraternité!
In the beginning was the Word . . .

For example, the ancient Hebrews believed that to say the name of their God aloud would cause injury, madness, or even death. Does this seem far-fetched? Let's look at an example from Stuart Chase's classic book, *The Power of Words:*

Fluorine in drinking water reduces tooth decay, especially in children. Certain fluorides are used in rat poisons. Newburgh, New York, voted to try fluoridation to improve the teeth of its children. The motion passed. Opposition to the project, despite a vigorous publicity campaign using the rat poison argument, was defeated. A day was announced when the chemical would be added to the water supply.

The day dawned, and before it was over, City Hall received hundreds of telephone calls complaining that the water was causing dizziness, nausea, headaches, and general debility. City Hall replied that, owing to technical problems, no fluoride had yet been added—it was the same old water.

Or consider another example that illustrates brilliantly the power and importance of language:

> The Japanese word "mokusatsu" has two meanings: to ignore and to refrain from comment. In July 1945, the Allies delivered the Potsdam ultimatum to Japan—"Surrender or be crushed." The Emperor of Japan and his cabinet wanted time to discuss terms and conditions and, therefore, issued a press release announcing a policy of "mokusatsu", meaning, "No comment at this time." Through a mix-up in translation, the foreign wires picked up the meaning, "The Emperor and cabinet ignore the demand to surrender."
>
> Had the correct meaning been picked up, there's a possibility that the war may have ended there—no Hiroshima or Nagasaki, no invasion of Manchuria, no Korean war. Thousands of young Americans and Japanese might have lived.

The language a group of people speaks imposes a unique view of nature, of existence, on those who speak it. The language learned from that culture provides an explanation of the universe, a "world view", and shapes how people think and experience the world. Let's look at some examples:

> The Sami language of Kiruna, Sweden, has 500 words for "snow" and several thousand for "reindeer." The Zulu tongues have 39 words for "green." None of these languages has a word for "computer."
>
> South Pacific Islanders have numerous words for "coconuts"; the Chinese and Japanese have a variety of words for "rice" and "tea"; the languages of India abound in words for "karma" and "reincarnation"; classical Arabic uses thousands of words to refer to a camel; Hindi numbers over 40 words for extended family relationships; Greeks have many words to express gratitude.
>
> The French have more nouns than many other languages. Is this predilection for concepts and idea words reflected in their heroes, their myths, and their way of life? The Germans have a highly inflected and compartmentalized language, a language that insists on strict word order. Could this reveal a need for discipline, predictability, and order? The Slavic and Arabic languages have an astounding number of descriptors, that is, adjectives and adverbs. Does this contribute to the length of much of their literatures?
>
> Adapted from Lustig & Koester, *Intercultural Competence*

In this chapter, we examine English, the dominant language of low-context cultures, and compare it to the Sino-Tibetan family of languages, which offers a particularly rich contrast.

I. ENGLISH: A LANGUAGE OF ACTION

Silence is the virtue of fools.

—AMERICAN PROVERB

If, in fact, language does provide a key to unlock the heart of a culture, what about the English language? What does English reveal? Let's consider the English language and its impact on culture.

English puts people at the center of the universe as the agents for action/decision (the subject of the sentence). What people do is interesting and important (the verb, for which there are over 90 forms). By clearly identifying who or what is affected by the action (direct and indirect objects), the linguistic structure of English captures how people affect the world.

Reality is measurable. Like most Indo-European languages, English reflects a belief in objective reality that can be understood through systematic observation, factual data, and logical proof. English prefers rational, linear, cause-and-effect thinking, anchored in space and time. Space is static, three-dimensional, and infinite. Time is kinetic, one-dimensional, flowing perpetually from past to present to future. Time is linear and the focus is on the future; change or progress is positive and of paramount importance because it proves the perfectibility of human life.

Individuals are responsible. The English language is structured to identify agent and action (the subject/verb dynamic), revealing an underlying belief in the value of achievement and individual responsibility. Most English speakers value action, prize competitiveness, and tend to regard thought and listening as passive, often negligible, occupations. Achievement is measured by outward signs of success: you are what you do, what you earn, what you possess. Failure is the nightmare of the American. The future (youth, progress, and change) matters more than the past (history, maturity, and stability).

Messages should be direct, explicit, and personal. English speakers like messages that are direct, linear, explicit, rational, and rich in content. They are less comfortable, if not downright uncomfortable, with silence. Presence is usually expressed through words. Opinions, perceptions, and feelings are what make people unique and interesting. Effective self-expression is, therefore, individualistic and direct, often focusing on abilities and achievements. The most frequently used words in English are "I" and "me."

> Because of a recent downsizing in a U.S. based airline, employees were offered out-placement services to help them with resumes, cover letters, and interviewing. Julia Patterson, one of the out-placement consultants, reported her experiences in assisting a manager with his resume and cover letter. In the first paragraph of his cover letter, the manager had used the personal pronoun "I" seventeen times when relating his accomplishments. "It was difficult to convince him to revise his sentences to focus on the prospective employer rather than on himself."

Let's compare the English language (the key to Anglo cultures) to the Sino-Tibetan family of languages—not just because this offers a particularly rich contrast, but also because these are cultures with which English speakers often do business.

II. SINO-TIBETAN LANGUAGES: A RICH CONTRAST

The speaker is a fool; the listener is wise.
—JAPANESE PROVERB

The Sino-Tibetan family of languages (spoken by most Asian cultures) is multi-valued, complex, and subtle, allowing for many shades of gray. There is no firm belief in objective reality; language seeks to capture impression, an overall emotional quality, and subjective, experiential thinking. Communication is fluid, indirect, inexplicit, nonlinear, and self-effacing.

As in most high-context cultures, people know and understand each other and their appropriate roles; words are not necessary to convey meaning. Many Asian cultures minimize verbal communication and are comfortable with silence, with the importance of words subordinated to that of presence.

Reality is complex and impressionistic.   Because the emphasis is impressionistic and organic, rather than rationalistic and analytical, thoughts about events and linguistic expressions of those thoughts often include both space and time, making verb tenses irrelevant or unnecessary. Words and sentences may be collapsed or shortened. Time is viewed as circular, not linear; repetitive, not progressive. "Nature" or "Life" is the center of the universe. The role of the individual is to live in harmony with nature, to coincide, merge, fuse to the greatest extent possible with the cycle of life—a cycle which is constant, never-ending, ever recreating itself.

> Many Hmong sayings are indirect. The Hmong believe that if the truth is spoken directly, evil spirits or unwanted guests can overhear it. Thus, a Hmong farmer might call out to his family, "Come sharpen your knives," rather than calling out, "It's time to eat," because the latter might attract evil spirits or animals who will eat up the meal.
>
> Adapted from Fadiman, *The Spirit Catches You and You Fall Down*

Messages should be indirect and impersonal.   In the absence of a firm belief in rational, verifiable reality, a strong emphasis on social and family relationships and loyalty to the group governs behavior. Religions—such as Confucianism, Shintoism, and Buddhism—support an orientation to collectivity, a philosophy that considers clear and well-defined relationships as the basis for society. People in these cultures value modesty and play down their own opinions, perceptions, or feelings; they seek social acceptance, confrontation-free relationships, and group harmony. In fact, the group is critical to one's self-definition, as T.R. Reid describes in *Confucius Lives Next Door:*

> The groups you belong to make up who you are. Your group is your identity. That's why the Japanese always introduce themselves with some group affiliation. It's never just "Hello, I'm Matsuda." That sentence would be considered wholly inadequate—and rude, to boot—because it doesn't convey the essential information. It's always "I'm Matsuda, of Tanigawa Sekiyu Inc." or "I'm Matsuda, of the class of 1923. . . ."

Harmony dominates.   It should come as no surprise, then, that direct expression of personal perceptions or opinions are usually avoided because they can disrupt group harmony. What is emphasized in the language is restraint, modesty, and self-deprecation (consider the Japanese proverb, "Boasting begins where wisdom stops"). "I" and "me" are used very infrequently; most sentences avoid personal pronouns altogether or use "we."

> Imi Ibayashi's manager in a Northeastern financial center called her into his office. "I thought I asked you to work on these numbers alone, but you keep talking about 'we' this and 'we' that. What's going on?" After consideration, Imi replied, "Yes, even though I worked on these numbers alone, I believe it is important to include our collective effort. Without you and the company, I would not even have this job."

III. GUIDELINES FOR USING LANGUAGE

Even the few examples we've discussed in this chapter illustrate the complexity and richness that language issues bring to the cultural "table." If the very structure of language influences the way people understand reality, then the picture of the universe shifts from language to language, and the way people conduct business shifts accordingly. The optimum solution, learning as many languages as possible, is both impractical and impossible.

Those who speak English are spared this task because the language of international business and government is English. About 1.4 billion people speak English as their second language—even though only about 400 million people speak it as their first language. Almost daily we learn that merged companies invariably select English as their common language. In fact, English has become so prevalent that "Global English" now comprises such disparate combinations as Anglonorsk (Norwegian English), Arablish (Arabic English), Chinglish (Chinese English), Franglais (French English), and Hindlish (Hindi English), to name but a few examples.

These facts, however, should not leave English speakers feeling complacent; they should empower English speakers to make every effort to use language effectively and sensitively to facilitate communication. But how can this be accomplished? The guidelines offered below point the way:

- *Be aware:* Non-native speakers of English are often unfamiliar with idiom and are confused by the shades of meaning of many English words. And non-English speakers may not reveal their confusion because many cultures consider questioning as impolite. Pretending to understand when you don't is often dictated by a culture's desire to be courteous, to seek harmony and confrontation-free relationships, and to avoid embarrassment. After all, needing to ask a question means that they didn't understand (thereby losing face) or that you did not do a good job explaining (potentially offensive or disrespectful to you).

- *Choose words carefully:* Words are powerful: they can hurt or support. To communicate cross-culturally, avoid words that disrespect or belittle others. Remember that jokes can also wound, especially the kind that make fun of a people or their beliefs. Finally, remember that many cultures that communicate indirectly may find directness rude or threatening.

- *Select simple, specific, concrete words:* Their meaning is clear, powerful, vivid, and, most importantly, unambiguous. Try to use common words, that is, words normally learned in the first two years of language study. Avoid uncommon words, such as "onus" for "burden," "jocose" for "witty," "efficacious" for "efficient," or "flux" for "continual change." Remember that English has about a billion words in its vocabulary—double that of any other language. (By way of comparison, Chinese has about 500 million and French 100 million words.)

- *Use the most common meaning of words:* Many words in English have multiple meanings. The word "high" has 20 meanings; the word "expensive" has only one. "Get" can mean to "buy, borrow, steal, rent, or retrieve." "Accurate" has only one meaning; "right" has 27. Non-native speakers of English are most likely to know only the first or second most common meaning.

- *Avoid idioms, slang, jargon, buzzwords, and acronyms:* These expressions are seldom taught in schools or in formal language courses. Using phrases like "What's going down?" or "Wassup?" (to ask what is happening), "Hang in there!" or "Keep on truckin!" (to encourage perseverance), and "What's the damage?" (to ascertain the cost) are certain prescriptives for misunderstanding. Avoid idioms that come from sport—"ballpark figure, slam dunk, out in left field, get to first base, run that by me, fish or cut bait, snookered, black-belt lean status"; expressions particular to the American culture—"raining cats and dogs, safe as Fort Knox, old as Methuselah, seat of the pants operation, keeping a low profile, the whole enchilada"; recent coinages—"legacy staff, fundage, webify, consumer-centricity"; and acronyms—"CYA, GIGO, WOMBAT."

- *Be sensitive when using new vocabulary:* The internet and new media have created countless terms that may be unfamiliar to your international business partner. Take a moment to explain or define the meaning of expressions like "TM shorthand," "DINK," "phishing," "chortal," "warez," and "backlink." For multicultural audiences, avoid trendy words unless you provide a definition.

- *Respect the basic rules of correct grammar and standard syntax:* Most people who learn English as a second language know their English grammar.

- *Be polite and formal:* People from many other cultures are not as casual as Americans. Be scrupulously polite. Avoid informality (e.g., use of first names) unless specifically invited to do so. Be aware that American "friendliness" is often misinterpreted as rudeness by cultures where form defines politeness.

- *Avoid jokes and humor:* Beware of sharing the latest joke. Humor, often based on word play, puns, or shared cultural references, is one of the most difficult things to translate. Also, remember that laughter in many cultures signifies embarrassment or nervousness.

- *Accommodate: meet your communication partner halfway:* Familiarize yourself with the accepted tone and reasoning style of the culture with which you are communicating; when your tone and style differ, your message may be misunderstood or negatively perceived. Being sensitive and making the necessary adjustment can go a long way toward building goodwill.

- *Develop empathy and patience:* Speak slowly, articulate carefully, use simple sentences, restate what you say in different words, and practice culturally-sensitive paraphrasing skills ("Please let me know if I have communicated clearly . . . Please correct me if I misinterpret what you have said . . .") to check for understanding. Remember that cultures that communicate indirectly may find directness aggressive.

- *Use several communication modes:* Ensure message clarity by using visual restatements (graphs, charts, tables) and written summaries, in addition to speaking.

- *Listen:* Listening is a very powerful communication tool: it involves putting aside your own self-interest so that you can step behind another's eyes and see things from that perspective. This is both a great compliment to the person with whom you're communicating as well as tangible proof of your commitment to understanding.

- *Value silence:* Try to become more comfortable with silence. Resolve to practice what the Chinese call "ting"—listening with ears, eyes, and heart, and not just "wun"—opening the door to the ears. Remember that many Asian cultures like periods of silence and do not like to be hurried. They view people who converse with no pauses as, at best, persons who have given little thought to what they are saying (as illustrated in the Indian proverb, "Where there's a glut of words, there's a dearth of intelligence") and, at worst, as insensitive bullies.

CHAPTER VI OUTLINE

CHAPTER VI

Writing

The pen wounds deeper than an arrow.
—YIDDISH PROVERB

The ground for cross-cultural miscommunication in written messages is fertile—from seemingly minor differences in writing dates and numbers, to the more egregious conclusions that a reader may form about a writer's actual ability to think clearly. Let's look at some examples:

A reader in Mexico City feels cold-shouldered and wounded by the American business letter that immediately opens with a direct statement of the problem, continues with possible solutions and recommendations, and ends with the terms and conditions surrounding the implementation of these solutions. Her culture and writing style mandate opening more personally, writing about their last meeting, inquiring about family and mutual friends, and setting a warmer tone for the discussion of the problem.

A business associate in Saudi Arabia is offended by the implication in a fax written by his American business partner that resolution of labor issues lies totally within his power. In his view of the world, Allah must be invoked: no one individual has the power or influence to solve major economic issues. In turn, his low-context business partner reacts negatively to the Saudi's inflated language.

A management consultant contracted to teach a certain number of courses in Beijing is horrified to learn that additional teaching responsibilities attach to her contract. She writes a clear, succinct, direct letter quoting from the contractual document and asking to be relieved of the ancillary responsibilities. The letter answering her request informs her that the situation has changed and her services will not be needed.

A U.S. applicant for a middle-management position with a Japanese bank writes an application letter that—he thinks—is powerful and convincing. His letter addresses all the stated requirements of the position and emphasizes his dominant role in expanding the client base and net worth of the investment portfolio at his previous position. After all, as the U.S. saying states, "Bragging saves advertising." Several weeks later, he receives a letter informing him that the position has already been filled.

The American vice president of a textile firm concludes that her manager in Indonesia cannot think clearly. Her judgment is based on the manager's "inability" to write in a direct, concise, and succinct manner about a simple delivery-scheduling problem. The Indonesian manager's response seems indirect, circuitous, and unfocused to the vice president.

These examples show that more is going on than words on paper. Even though more than 98% of all international business correspondence is in English, the readers in the examples given above are "reading between the lines." The messages are not being interpreted correctly because of a cultural disconnect; diverse cultural outlooks are interfering with the clarity of the written message. To develop an understanding of how written messages can be misinterpreted, we must acquire a better sense of what different cultures require and expect.

This chapter will map the different preferences of various cultures.

I. PREFERRED CHANNEL

"Put it in writing!"

English communicators often choose writing as a preferred communication channel. The business environment in the United States, Canada, Western Europe, Australia, and New Zealand is often litigious, and business organizations are becoming more complex. Clear, detailed written contracts are a must in the face of increased government regulation and the threat of consumer lawsuits.

English-speaking cultures are results driven, thus new technologies, systems, and products are quickly espoused and used as soon as they come off the assembly line. And because telephonic and high-speed connections are rapid and relatively inexpensive in the United States and most of Western Europe, technology appears the ideal answer in the quest for efficiency.

"Please call if you have any questions," is a common tag line in business letters in the U.S. However, such an invitation is likely to be regarded as dismissive in relational cultures such as Nigeria. Iyiola Obayomi, the manager of a bank in Lagos reported, "I want to see the person with whom I am dealing. There is no substitute."

Communicators from other cultures may prefer other channels. Consider the cultures we're been describing and discussing—the importance an Italian, a Greek, or a Saudi places on relationships and feelings; the critical roles that context, harmony, and formality play for an Indonesian or a Malay. These cultures rely less on written contracts and may not readily accept the challenges technology poses. Furthermore, the cost of technology may preclude widespread usage in India, many Southeast Asian countries, Africa, and much of South America. These cultures often prefer a personal call to a written document; as the Turkish proverb explains, "A cup of coffee commits one to 40 years of friendship."

II. DIRECTNESS

The squeaky wheel gets the grease.
—U.S. PROVERB

English language writers value direct messages.   As we've discussed previously, English language writers like direct messages. "What's the big news?" "How does it affect me?" "What must I do?" Business writers are taught to know when something needs to be "put in writing" and to communicate ideas, thoughts, or observations directly, as facts.

Getting straight to the point as quickly as possible is viewed as proof of sincerity and openness and, furthermore, as evidence that you have nothing to hide. This approach is also perceived as respectful to readers—you're not wasting their time. Thus, business communication courses and textbooks advocate placing the main message—the issue, conclusions, and recommendation—in the first paragraph or (and this is an American invention) beginning the document with an executive summary.

> The "sage" of Omaha and one of the richest investors in the U.S., Warren Buffet, collaborated with then SEC (U.S. Securities and Exchange Commission) Chairman, Arthur Levitt, to devise "Plain English" rules for the writing of U.S. business disclosure documents. The advice given in *A Plain English Handbook* includes the following: short sentences; definite, concrete, everyday words; active voice; and bullet lists. The rules prohibit legal jargon or highly technical business terms and the use of multiple negatives. In his introduction, Levitt advises businesspeople to "Tell them plainly what they need to know to make intelligent investment decisions."

The English language is dynamic, capturing the cultural value of individual action and achievement through the active voice and the Who/Did/What/to Whom or to What sentence pattern. This pattern puts people at the center of the universe and illustrates a core belief in the value of doing (not just being).

Writers of other languages prefer indirect messages.   Because writers in other cultures value relationships over a purely transactional business model, they may not place as great a value on directness. They may, in fact, find the direct approach abrupt, rude, and unfriendly, the output of people who don't want or value relationships, who only want to do business.

- *Southern European, Mediterranean, Central and South American cultures* consider business transactions less important than human feelings. For them, the written message is a substitute for personal contact, and nurturing the relationship is more important than the rapid, efficient delivery of facts or ideas. As a result, the direct, English language approach—immediately and without preamble identifying the issue to be discussed—appears abrupt, unfriendly, and impersonal. People from these cultures prefer written messages that fulfill a social as well as a business role: evoking the existing relationship, recalling the last meeting, inquiring after children and family members, and maintaining a warm and highly personal tone.

    A letter from a health organization in Sao Paulo, Brazil, to a U.S. business that donated funds for a dental clinic began as follows: "Dear Honored Sponsor, We will offer manifest feelings of appreciation for the financial support you have provided to our dental clinic. Many lives here will be touched by your generosity."

- *Arabic countries,* especially those that adhere to Islam, find directness pagan and uncivilized. Their written messages frequently begin by invoking Allah's blessing on the reader and his family and end by saying, "Do this for my sake." The comment acknowledges that the speaker will be obligated to return the favor. In other words, written requests carry the weight of reciprocity.

    A letter from a trade minister in Saudi Arabia to a partner in the U.S. began with "Greetings of Allah to you and all those for whom you care," and ended with "We ask that you do the requested favor for our sake, and we invoke the blessings of Allah on you and your endeavors."

- *Asian cultures,* reflecting their belief that people must live in harmony with nature, often begin their written communication with descriptions of the season and its beauty and bounty.

    A letter containing an order from a Japanese buyer of industrial batteries to a U.S. supplier began, "Our fall colors are beginning to be seen. The maple trees are brilliantly red with the hint of colder weather that will soon arrive."

III. IMMEDIACY

The early bird gets the worm.
—AMERICAN PROVERB

English writers prefer immediate messages. English-speaking writers value time, and most business writing courses exhort us not to waste the time of our readers. Business writers are exhorted to write immediately because delays may worsen the situation and silence may be interpreted as concurrence. Writing immediately is also viewed as respect for time.

Writers of other languages may delay writing. Other cultures measure time differently and place much emphasis on context and relationships.

- *Southern European, Mediterranean, Central, and South American cultures:* Because these cultures value feelings over business contracts, they may delay writing immediately about problems. They may allow time to cast further light on an issue or to diffuse a situation, which may cause embarrassment or pain to responsible individuals.

- *Arabic cultures:* The U.S. and other low-context cultures' emphasis on immediacy is directly related to a belief in personal responsibility. This flies in the face of the Muslim belief prevalent in many Arabic cultures that no human being has the power to control events.

- *Asian cultures:* Communicators from Asian cultures may circle around issues, contemplating the context, considering relationships, allowing time for reflection, and pondering possible links with similar problems in the past. They often interpret our emphasis on immediacy as simplistic. Consider the Taoist proverb, "No one can see their reflection in running water. It is only in still water that we can see clearly."

IV. CLARITY AND CONCISENESS

Spend words as efficiently as money.

—OKINAWAN PROVERB

English language writers value clear, concise writing. Writers in low-context cultures (discussed in Chapter 2), value precise and complete information. Historically, such cultures believe that thinking is mainly a verbal activity and that writing can support the thought process. In other words, good writing is not possible without clear thinking. Conversely, the effort to write well (it is believed) encourages logical reasoning.

Business writing courses emphasize making messages clear and concrete because vague or abstract messages are ambiguous. Thus, words that capture exact and precise meaning, words that are specific, precise, and simple are considered preferable to general or category words that are hard to measure. Business writers are taught to avoid circuitousness and to write concisely, eliminating long sentences.

Writers of other languages place less emphasis on clarity and conciseness. Because writers from other cultures rely more heavily on context than on linguistic messaging to capture meaning, their messages may seem circuitous.

- *Southern European, Mediterranean, Central, and South American cultures:* Business communicators from Southern European, Mediterranean, Central, and South American cultures often favor lengthy, flowery, and overly qualified sentences. This may not only be a carry-over from their mother tongues—the Romance languages—but may also demonstrate a desire to spare the feelings and dignity of others. Ambiguity and indirectness diffuse responsibility and can mean that the writer is taking care not to accuse or blame. Furthermore, what U.S. writers consider digressions or tangential information can supply bits of circumstance or situational description that clarify the context.

- *Arabic cultures:* Arabs value their language and exult in demonstrating their knowledge of vocabulary: "Nothing done with intelligence is done without words" (Arab proverb). The scholar Edward Said explains that Arabic speakers regard their language as "sihr halal"—a legitimate magic or sorcery, a gift from Allah because the Koran is written in Arabic. This can, and often does, lead to the use of words for effect and not just for concrete meaning. Clarity and conciseness take a back seat to exuberance and exaggeration, and length of writing is not judged negatively. As Samovar and Porter point out in *Communication Between Cultures,* an Arabic statement can run to 100 words when English would use ten.

• *Asian cultures:* Clarity and conciseness have little meaning in Asian cultures because there is a general mistrust of words ("Those who speak do not know, those who know do not speak.") This attitude is understandable in cultures that value harmony, listening, contemplation, and the preservation of dignity and "face." Many Asian businesspeople express themselves through understatement and view bluntness as unsophisticated and crass. Add to that the Asian belief that the "truth" is not objective-that it can only be grasped in context, through association, and by understanding the cyclical nature of life-and clarity and conciseness recede in importance.

V. GUIDELINES FOR WRITING ACROSS CULTURES

In addition to the ideas provided in the previous chapter on language, the following guidelines should help you produce more effective written communication for partners and associates in other cultures:

- *Adjust your writing style:* Although you may find it challenging to adopt the style of a different culture, making even minor adjustments can make an enormous difference in how your message is received. Remember that other cultures may not value directness or immediacy and may define clarity differently. Writing that seems indirect, circuitous, and unfocused may result from the culture's avoidance of blame and focus on circumstance, context, and "face."

  Consider beginning your written communication with a more personal opening, providing context to statements or analyses, and avoiding requests to assign responsibility or to blame individuals.

- *Become familiar with patterns of logic and organization used in other cultures:* Businesspeople from East Asian cultures may not organize information linearly, but relationally, targeting the correspondences between various elements. The Japanese may stress on rapport. Writers from Mediterranean cultures often devote the whole beginning section of a document to tracing and commemorating the history of the relationship. The Germans use chronology when arranging and presenting ideas; they give the background first and position recommendations at the end. The French take pride in style and rhetorical elegance.

  Adjusting to your reader's pattern of logic and organizational flow can go a long way to making your written document more accessible and successful.

- *Use technology with care:* Many American businesspeople have found that the personal call is a requisite for successful intercultural business dealings—it is tangible proof of goodwill and personal commitment to the business relationship. Others report better results with telephone calls and letters than with email. If you do use electronic media, familiarize yourself with appropriate discourse etiquette for the particular culture and reader.

  The key seems to be to establish the relationship on a sound footing; once it's in place, the misunderstandings and discomforts caused by technological issues diminish significantly.

- *Make your written documents accessible and reader-friendly by*
  1. Increasing white space: Many cultures prefer double-spacing, indentation, and more space for notes and translation.
  2. Using headings and subheadings: Although important in all business writing because they permit rapid location of information, they're critical when communicating with nonnative speakers.
  3. Verifying titles and spelling of names: These mistakes reflect carelessness, rudeness, and lack of goodwill.
  4. Being careful with dates and times: U.S. writers use the month/day/year order; Europeans prefer day/month/year. Avoid ambiguity and misunderstanding by writing out the month. Many countries and the U.S. military operate on a 24-hour clock, so provide the equivalent to 2:00 p.m. as 1400 hours.
  5. Being careful with measurements and temperature: Since much of the world uses the metric system, give the metric equivalents in parentheses for distances, weights and volumes. Use both Fahrenheit and Celsius when citing temperatures.
  6. Punctuating large numbers carefully: Note the use of commas and periods in the following example: 5,426.24 becomes 5.426,24 in many countries. Note also that there's a difference in the use of the number *billion:* some countries define it as one followed by nine zeros; others as one followed by 12 zeros.

7. Avoiding abbreviations and acronyms, especially new technical additions: Non-native readers may not be familiar with abbreviations and acronyms like LCD, PDA, or DRM.

Although native speakers of English begin with an edge—their native language is the language of international business—this can be both a blessing and a curse. A blessing because English speakers need not spend much time learning this communication vehicle. A curse because, unless English speakers become aware and remain constantly sensitive to the possible pitfalls, they can wound their multicultural business partners, damage the business relationship, and create a sizeable web of misunderstanding.

CHAPTER VII OUTLINE

CHAPTER VII

Communicating Nonverbally

Whatever is written on the face is always seen.
—PALESTINIAN PROVERB

Knowledge of nonverbal communication is crucial to success when communicating across cultures. Communicating nonverbally involves the many aspects of communication that convey meaning without words. Researchers have estimated that anywhere from 65 to 90% of communication is nonverbal with the importance of this type of communication varying widely across cultures.

Nonverbal communication includes eye contact, facial expression, hand gestures, the use of physical space, and silence. The culture's relative attitude toward time is also indicative of nonverbal communication. As the following scenario highlights, an international reception is a great place to observe various aspects of nonverbal communication.

Molly Henderson and her colleague Hans Schimmel attended a reception in Boston that kicked off a weekend of meetings. VMF Construction Company had formed a partnership with two multinational firms to design and build a medical center in South Africa. Of the 25 people at the reception, only five were born in the United States; the others represented various world cultures. After the reception, Molly and Hans met to debrief and to share their impressions.

Hans complained that the Argentinean team had arrived very late. Molly noted that at one point Mr. Al-Jezal had backed the Londoner, Dr. James Lennon, into a corner of the room. "It was like a dance," she reported, "and Dr. Lennon looked uncomfortable."

Hans had observed one of the Korean attendees, "Well, he wasn't the only one who was distressed. I kept trying to catch Mr. Park's eye, but it seemed to make him so uncomfortable. When I would ask him a question, there would be long pauses before he answered."

"Did you see those two guys wearing tuxedos?" asked Molly. "Why would anybody think a business reception would be formal? I just don't understand why things didn't go better. I sure hope the actual meetings are smoother than the reception. At least they all speak English."

Molly and Hans were experiencing a common phenomenon when doing business in the 21st century. English may be the language of business, but nonverbal cues can totally change the meaning of a word or phrase. In the following sections, we'll examine aspects of nonverbal communication that can affect the outcome of business transactions across cultures.

I. EYE CONTACT

Like other aspects of nonverbal communication, eye contact affects both the sending and receiving of messages.

A renowned Japanese economist traveled to the United States to speak to business groups and to meet with economists from several universities. At one meeting, Dr. Takahashi enjoyed lunch with a distinguished group of businesspeople and then made a few remarks in perfect English. Dr. Takahashi squeezed his eyes shut as he spoke. Occasionally, he would open his eyes slightly only to squeeze them shut again. This nonverbal behavior prompted several people to wonder, "Was he hiding something?" or "Do you think he was nervous?" It was neither. Like many Asian cultures, the Japanese are taught to avoid direct eye contact with strangers. Dr. Takahashi was simply communicating in a way that was more comfortable for him.

One of the earliest learned behaviors in any culture is the proper use of eye contact. Most of us are unaware of our eye placement during communication because we have internalized what we were taught about proper eye behaviors from childhood. What we don't realize is that eye placement not only differs *across* cultures, but eye behavior for listening differs from eye behavior for speaking *within* cultures. Adding to the confusion when communicating cross-culturally, eye placement differs when communicating upward or downward in the social hierarchy. In the following section, we'll examine some of these invisible rules.

Speaking vs. listening eye behavior: Many research studies have shown that eye behavior may differ when speaking and listening. These differences can occur within subcultures even when people live in the same geographic area.

- *Euro-American culture:* One study showed that speakers from the Euro-American culture do not usually maintain direct and constant eye contact when speaking. Rather, they tend to look away as they speak and only glance back every so often to check the listener's eye contact. The direct gaze of the listener assures the speaker that careful listening is occurring. In other words, Euro-Americans have generally been taught that the listener should be looking at them very intently. Most Euro-Americans become very annoyed when others do not maintain "proper" listening eye contact.

As a newly promoted marketing manager, Martha Blanchard attended a business convention of cell phone industry representatives in Vail, Colorado. When she returned, she talked with a colleague about the conference—especially the opening and closing receptions. "People were so rude," she remarked, "They never listened even when they asked me a direct question. They were always scanning the room to find someone more important to talk to."

Martha experienced a phenomenon common in business even when communicating with people who have the same cultural roots. Although Euro-Americans have learned the "proper" listening behavior (i.e., eyes on the speaker), many people break the rule and, therefore, appear inattentive or rude.

- *African-American culture:* Research has also shown that African Americans may use eye contact differently from Euro-Americans when speaking and listening. One researcher found that African Americans tend to look intently while speaking. However, instead of looking steadily while listening, the African American may look at the speaker and then look down or away when listening. Imagine the possible confusion when an African-American manager is speaking to a Euro-American manager, and their eye contact is out of synch! Each may believe there is something "wrong" without knowing the cause. In such an occurrence, it is important to discuss openly the perceptions of each participant in the communication to clarify intent and meaning.

Direct or indirect eye contact: World travelers learn that if they don't quickly adapt to the use of direct or indirect eye contact in the culture they are visiting, they could invite trouble. An Arab proverb states, "The eyes are the windows of the soul," and those from Arab cultures value direct and constant eye contact as the keystone of good communication. Cross-cultural communicators soon learn to adjust the directness of their eye contact to match their surroundings as the following illustrates.

A Lebanese trader arrived in New York for meetings with buyers of rugs and carpets. During his ride on the subway, he gazed at all the interesting people. Suddenly, another rider accosted him. "What are *you* looking at?" Mr. Al-Batal had no idea what the man was talking about because he was unaware that he had done anything unusual. When he arrived at his appointment, he asked one of the buyers about the man's accusatory question. He was told that people in the United States tend to glance only furtively at strangers. The American culture teaches that direct gazing is intrusive and threatening.

On the advice of the buyer, Mr. Al-Batal learned to cast his eyes downward or look at a newspaper as he rode the subway or walked the streets of New York. If he looked at others, he learned to glance quickly and never to look a stranger in the eye.

Even within the greater culture, subcultures may have different preferences in eye placement that can lead to many misunderstandings.

- *Native-American and Asian cultures:* A Native-American or Asian child is taught to lower the eyes when listening to an elder such as a teacher. Eyes cast downward indicate both appropriate listening behavior and respect for the elder. Looking directly at an elder would constitute bad manners, challenge, or even hostility.

- *Euro-American culture:* Many people from Northern European backgrounds can remember being told by their parents, "Look at me when I'm talking to you!" Children are taught to look directly at their elders to show respect and the proper listening behavior. To Euro-Americans, a child looking at the floor would be telegraphing shame or hostility—not polite listening behavior. These learned eye behaviors can carry over to adulthood and negatively affect workplace communication if they are not expected and understood.

Social hierarchy and eye contact: Social hierarchy can influence the choice of direct or indirect eye placement. Direct eye contact often indicates that communication is occurring between equals. Indirect eye behaviors can indicate respect for someone upward in the hierarchy, especially in cultures where there is a clearly defined power structure (as we explain in Chapter 5).

When accountant Vincent Rodrigue received his six-month performance review at a national bank in the U.S., he was surprised to read, "Mr. Rodrigue does not maintain proper eye contact during discussions with his manager." As a young employee in Haiti, Vincent had always been careful to avoid a constant, direct gaze when talking with the manager. He had been taught that he should look down while listening to show proper respect.

In an open discussion with his manager, Vincent was able to discuss the problem. Because he was a valuable employee who showed promise, the company hired a communication coach to teach Vincent the expected eye behavior of his new corporate culture. On return business trips to Haiti, however, Vincent again showed proper respect for his elders by looking downward when being addressed.

Just as he was comfortable speaking two languages fluently, he had learned that he had to become just as "fluent" in nonverbal communication to be successful.

Knowing that eye placement behaviors vary widely across cultures will help the international businessperson avoid incorrect or negative assumptions and will benefit the intercultural communication process.

II. FACIAL EXPRESSION

Facial expressions vary greatly across cultures as they convey many emotions such as anger, happiness, sadness, and surprise. To illustrate this variety, we discuss two aspects of facial expression—the smile and the nod. The following example shows the difficulties in conveying meaning nonverbally across cultures.

> Margie Choi has an undergraduate degree in marketing and is pursuing an MBA. She recently completed an internship with a large advertising firm in the Northeast. On returning to her campus, she made an appointment with a former professor who had helped her secure the internship. "I think they hated my final presentation," she lamented. "They sat there and stared at me, and no one nodded. Maybe they didn't understand me because of my accent."
>
> Since the professor had already received a favorable report from the advertising firm, she was able to reassure Ms. Choi that her presentation was well received. The Euro-American managers sat stony-faced because that is part of their business culture—to mask emotions. Their lack of facial expression was neither an affirmation nor a condemnation of her performance. In fact, they were very pleased with Ms. Choi's assistance in landing a large account with a Korean firm and had made plans to offer her a full time position when she graduates.

Nodding: As the example above illustrates, nodding can vary in meaning in across cultures.

- *As a way of agreeing or disagreeing:* When U.S. businesspeople were asked to interpret the head nodding of others, most selected the meaning, "I agree with you." But in Bulgaria, for example, nodding indicates a negative rather than a positive response. In Turkey, a quick lifting of the chin accompanied by a tongue click indicates disapproval.

- *As a listening tool:* Be aware, also, of the possible misinterpretations of using nodding as a listening tool. In different cultures, nodding may indicate (1) I'm listening, and I agree; (2) I'm listening, but I don't necessarily agree; (3) I'm very confused, but I want you to keep talking, so I can try to figure out what you are saying; or (4) I'm trying to encourage you by providing positive nonverbal feedback.

Smiling: Smiling is another example of nonverbal communication that varies across cultures. Although babies in all cultures smile, children are taught the proper use of the smile and its natural extension, the laugh, as they mature.

- *Multiple meanings:* The smile may have multiple meanings depending on the culture. In some cultures, smiles can indicate fear; a smile can be a method of disarming a possible aggressor. In other cultures, the smile can indicate friendliness. In still other cultures, smiles may indicate nervousness or embarrassment. In the U.S. culture, smiles have many meanings, including pleasure, friendliness, and amusement, but a smile or laugh does not usually indicate fear or embarrassment as it might in many Asian cultures.

  > An American consultant was delayed in meeting her clients in Hong Kong by a telephone call from home informing her that her mother's illness had been diagnosed as cancer. Wishing to apologize for her lateness, she informed her clients of the reason; they reacted to the information by giggling. The consultant was profoundly shocked and angered by this seemingly callous response.
  >
  > Months later, when she came to know some of her clients personally, she learned that their response was one of nervous embarrassment—they had not known how to react to such intimate and dismaying personal information.

- *Different frequencies:* In addition to carrying different meanings, smiles vary in frequency across cultures. For example, the French are masters of the *mine d'enterrement* (funereal expression) and don't smile without a reason, whereas in the U.S., people may smile frequently at perfect strangers to indicate they mean no harm.

To be successful communicating across cultures, it's important to observe and mirror the use of the smile in the other culture. Being able to interpret its frequency and meaning will help you avoid misunderstandings and communicate more effectively.

III. HAND GESTURES

Baseball, the great "American" pastime, is one of the best places to observe the use of word signs—hand gestures that stand for a particular word. While some are obvious, such as holding the hand in front with the palm facing away from the body to mean "stop," others are not so obvious. The manager uses a series of complicated signals such as chin taps, head rubs, belly scratches, and ear pulls to telegraph the next play to the batter. Catchers use hand signals to the pitcher to indicate the type of pitch such as fastball, curve ball, or sinker. The signal also indicates the direction of the pitch—inside, over the plate, or outside.

An interesting and relatively recent addition to nonverbal communication in baseball involves greeting behaviors between players, such as double high fives (hand slapping), elbow bumping, jumping, and chest thumping in an elaborately timed choreography.

Finally, a homerun hitter may use nonverbal communication to signal his thanks to a spiritual entity (one player places fingers to lips, then hand over heart, and finally finger pointing to the sky). The batter may also "thank" the crowd with a pointed finger and then a fist over the heart.

In this section, we'll look at the various ways different cultures use their hands in nonverbal communication.

Gestures: Like touching, the use of the hands to gesture varies across cultures. It is dangerous to assume that the use or lack of gestures has the same importance as it does in your own culture. Our advice is to observe the size and type of gestures within the context of a conversation or meeting and use few gestures until you are certain they will be correctly understood by the other culture.

- *Broad or small gestures:* In some cultures, the use of large gestures may indicate a person of importance. In others, large gestures may indicate someone with little refinement. It is dangerous to assume that the use of or lack of gestures has the same importance as it does for your own culture. For example, the use of broad gestures may be annoying, irritating, and distracting when communicating with someone from Asia where small gestures are preferred. On the other hand, someone from a Latino or Mediterranean culture might find a lack of broad gestures puzzling and, therefore, may doubt the confidence of the speaker. Neither of these assumptions is necessarily correct. The relative use or non-use of broad gestures is usually consistent within the greater culture.

- *Same gesture, different meaning:* The specific meaning of gestures also varies among cultures. Here are some examples: (1) *OK sign:* In the U.S., the OK sign (thumb and finger circle) signals that everything is going well. However, the same sign is considered vulgar in such varied cultures as Paraguay, Singapore, and Russia. In France, a similar gesture means "nothing" or "zero" as in, "that idea is worthless." (2) *Thumbs up:* Similarly, the "thumbs up" gesture has a negative meaning in the Middle East where the thumb should never be used alone in gesturing. (3) *Use of the left hand:* The left hand is considered unclean in both Muslim and Hindu cultures, and, therefore, any gesture with the left hand during a business presentation may be considered rude. (4) *Beckoning gestures:* In the U.S. people beckon with the palm upward and the fingers scooping and curling repeatedly. In other cultures such as Pakistan, a person who is beckoning another would orient the palm downward with fingers waving toward the body. (5) *Pointing:* Pointing with one finger at another person during a presentation is ill advised in many cultures, as the following example demonstrates.

> During his presidency, Bill Clinton traveled to China and, at one stop during the trip, spoke to university students in Beijing. President Clinton's remarks were generally well received and were followed by a lively question and answer session.
>
> When interviewed for the American press, one student remarked, "During the question and answer period, I did not understand why the president pointed his finger at us to select a person. We would not use such a rude gesture." Puzzled, the American reporter asked the student what gesture the president should have used. The student answered using a sweep of the open hand—palm upward.

- *Posture and body language:* Posture is another area where cultural differences can cause miscommunication. In some cultures such as France, executives and government officials are expected to sit with erect posture. In the U.S., however, a slouching posture can simply mean that a person is relaxed regardless of their position in society.

  A generally slumping posture and slow walk with head cast downward can indicate someone who is troubled or sad in many cultures. Likewise a shrug of the shoulders can indicate, "I don't know." Turning away from someone as they speak or crossing the arms can mean that the receiver is rejecting an idea.

Men and women tend to adjust their body posture differently. Women in the United States are more likely to face each other as they speak. Men tend to stand beside each other as they speak unless they are angry or showing aggressiveness.

To avoid problems, businesspeople who want to communicate effectively across cultures should observe carefully and keep their hand gestures to a minimum until they learn the other culture's preferences.

Touching: Communicating nonverbally also involves touching. In some cultures, it is impossible to communicate successfully one-on-one without touching the other person: in Latino cultures, touching is a natural part of any communication exchange with many contacts per conversation. In Northern European cultures, touching is less common: men tend not to touch other men while talking in a business context in the United States. In other cultures, touching is permitted or forbidden, depending on the gender—Arab cultures forbid touching women, but Arab men touch each other often when conversing.

To communicate effectively across cultures, observe carefully the nonverbal touching behaviors of those from that culture. Until you become acquainted with the acceptable touching behaviors of the other culture, the best advice is to "keep your hands to yourself."

IV. SPACE

Toddlers in all cultures are like puppies in their use of physical space. They stand close enough to touch, roll around, and step on each other's feet. As children grow, they are taught how to greet each other and how to maintain an appropriate conversational distance. These spatial customs vary widely across cultures; knowledge about use of space can influence the success of cross-cultural business communication.

Greeting behavior: The use of space in greeting behavior will usually be consistent with other nonverbal communication within that culture.

- *Bowing:* In Japan, the person of lower rank performs a lower bow than the person of higher rank. Bowing is such an integral part of proper greeting behavior that is not uncommon to see businesspeople in Tokyo bowing as they speak to the other person by cell phone.

- *Hands together:* In the Hindu culture, the "namaste" gesture (hands together and head quickly bowed) indicates respect for someone of rank. The Thai "wai" and the Laotian "nop" have similar appearances and functions, although people from these cultures can easily spot the differences.

- *Handshakes:* While hearty handshakes may be the norm in such cultures as the Netherlands and the U.S., a gentler, lighter handshake is customary in France, India, and many Asian countries.

- *Kissing:* Some of the Mediterranean cultures practice the "abrazo" in greeting people of either sex, which can involve hugs and shoulder pats. In addition, some Slavic and European cultures "air kiss" on alternating cheeks.

Just as when you learn a new dance step, the trick is to follow the lead of your business counterpart. Soon, you'll know the exact number and intensity of kisses, hugs, and handshakes.

Conversational distance: Once the greeting is completed, it's necessary to figure out how close to stand to each other. What one culture would consider an appropriate conversational distance, another might interpret as aggressive or possibly intimate. Therefore, it's critical for the well-informed businessperson to know the spatial needs of the other culture and to flex to those needs. If we stand still and allow the other person to establish the communication distance, we will be more successful in cross-cultural exchanges. Sitting down can be a welcome relief for those whose cultures require quite different conversational distances because the position of the furniture helps build an appropriate speaking distance.

Businesspeople from British cultures are taught to prefer a large speaking distance—as much as 3 or 4 feet in public areas. In the Arab culture where all the senses are used in communicating, people are taught to stand very close—18 inches or less. Each communicator should bathe in the breath of the other, and touching among men is common as the following example shows.

> The late Saudi Arabian King Fahd bin Abdul Aziz received petitioners in an event filmed by an American news network. The King sat in a throne-like chair with the petitioner on an ottoman in front of him. The faces of the two men were less than 20 inches apart, and their eyes locked as one spoke and the other listened. As he spoke, the petitioner held the hand of his king and patted it several times.

The ability to communicate effectively by respecting another businessperson's preferred space becomes easier with time. However, it takes both knowledge and determination to achieve effective and culture-appropriate use of conversational distance.

Office space: Another aspect of the space around us is the size and layout of offices. The placement of desks in a large room can indicate many things. In a hierarchical culture, it can indicate a lack of prestige. However, in collective cultures, it is a powerful nonverbal message that the employees are a team working together on their projects. A sensitive cross-cultural communicator will observe nonjudgmentally to determine the meaning of office layout and space.

Dress and accessories: What you wear also sends a nonverbal signal. We follow appropriate dress codes at work, wearing either business suits or business casual attire. The care with which we prepare ourselves to enter the workday indicates a certain respect for the job and our coworkers. Appropriate attire for business situations varies widely across cultures and can be a source of miscommunication when ignored.

> Texas agronomist Tom Goodroy was invited to Mexico to share technical information with a farmer's co-op. Used to wearing jeans and a western shirt, he was unsure of how to dress for the trip. He asked the

advice of an expert in cross-cultural communication and was told to
wear a suit on the plane so that he would be appropriately attired and
thus respectful of the representatives who would meet him at the air-
port and escort him to his meetings. Tom was skeptical. . . . After all,
he would be meeting with a bunch of farmers.

On his return, Tom called the consultant and said, "You were
right about wearing the suit. Even the taxi drivers wore ties!" His trip
was a success, and both his verbal and nonverbal messages were well
received.

Physical attire also includes accessories such as jewelry or head cov-
erings. In many Arab cultures, the arms, legs, and torso should be entirely covered. And in some cultures, national or religious symbols
on jewelry or clothing can send a nonverbal message of disrespect.
Gender preferences in attire can also be extreme, so it's important to
ask questions about the appropriate attire for business meetings that
involve interaction with other cultures.

Time: As we discussed in detail in Chapter 3, the attitude toward
time is an important consideration when learning about culture.
Some cultures (the U.S. and Northern Europe) believe that life is
lived by the clock, and that every minute saved during the day is precious. In these cultures, being on time is extremely important.
Without a word being spoken, those who are late are deemed disrespectful, lazy, or disorganized. Other cultures (many Latin American
and Mediterranean nations) have a more relaxed view of time. How
late people are is merely part of the flow of events and does not
necessarily carry a negative nonverbal message. We advise businesspeople to be on time until they can clearly establish the other culture's time preferences.

V. SILENCE AND THE RHYTHM OF LANGUAGE

Silence and the rhythm of language vary depending on what the culture teaches. That is, the appropriate pause between a question and an answer or a statement and a response can vary widely. In some cultures, verbal communication overlaps. In other cultures, there may be one second or several seconds between question and answer or statement and response. The silence—or lack of it—is a powerful part of nonverbal communication.

For example, when you observe two people speaking Spanish, there will probably be overlap between words, sentences, or change of speaker. One speaker begins before the other finishes. When you observe two people speaking Mandarin, you may notice more space or silence between one sentence and the next. Being aware of the sometimes-conflicting meaning of silence can help businesspeople communicate across cultures.

- *Silence is negative and indicates confusion:* Because Euro-Americans and Northern Europeans expect a certain rhythm and cadence of statement and response, they may interpret silence as confusion about the statement, as a negative response to the proposed idea, or even as anger at the speaker or the proposal.

- *Silence is positive and indicates respect:* People from Asian cultures use silence to indicate respect for the other speaker, consideration for the idea the speaker has presented, and time to weigh the pros and cons of the statement and form a thoughtful response.

  During the 20th century, a series of movies featured an Asian-American detective named Charlie Chan. The typical Americans who encountered the Confucian character described him as "inscrutable." Even today, many Euro-American businesspeople do not understand the Asian culture's use of silence. The Asian proverb, "Listen a hundred times, ponder a thousand times, speak little," emphasizes a strong preference for nonverbal communication.

Impact of silence on intercultural communication: Notice that people from the United States and many European cultures interpret silence in negative ways, whereas those from the Asian cultures tend to interpret silence as respectful and positive. Imagine international negotiators representing these cultures sitting across the table from each other. The Euro-Americans present an offer. The Asians silently consider the offer. The Euro-Americans interpret the silence as a rejection of their offer, and the Asians are surprised when they almost immediately receive a better offer. No wonder there is sometimes mistrust and confusion when these cultures discuss business.

> Businesspeople at breakout sessions of a conference on managing in the 21st century attended a series of panel discussions on cross-cultural communication. Each panel represented a major world culture. The use of silence by the Asian panel members surprised the Euro-American attendees even though they had been instructed to notice it as a pertinent feature of Asian nonverbal communication. One participant remarked that the Asian panel, made up of speakers from Japan, Korea, and China, would consider the question for several long moments and then look at each other politely before one of them would speak. Each person on the panel had a chance to answer every question unlike some of the other panels, where speakers often interrupted each other's remarks.

VI. GUIDELINES

Careful observation is the secret to effective nonverbal communication across cultures. As you observe, be aware of the countless ways a culture may communicate nonverbally. When in doubt, seek the advice of local communication consultants.

- *Eye contact:* Avoid making negative assumptions about differences in eye contact. When in doubt about the nonverbal communication of your international business associate, ask questions to verbally clarify meaning. Try to mirror the culture's use of direct or indirect eye contact.

- *Facial expressions:* Be aware that facial expressions convey meaning and that these meanings vary across cultures. Observe the use of nodding and smiling, and do not assume a positive or negative opinion from a facial expression until you are sure of its meaning.

- *Gestures:* Since the use of gestures varies widely across cultures, keep gestures small until you are sure of the preferences of the other culture. If you have a doubt about a gesture or word sign used by the other businessperson, ask for clarification. Don't assume that any gesture has universal meaning.

- *Posture and body language:* Observe the posture and body language of your counterparts in cross-cultural communication.

Once you are sure of the intended nonverbal meaning, mirror their posture and body language to the extent that you can do so comfortably.

- *Touching:* Avoid touching others until you are sure of the "rules" for touching behaviors.

- *Greeting behavior:* Do not initiate kissing or embracing until you are certain of the appropriate greeting behaviors of the other culture. On the other hand, try not to back away if someone from a different culture greets you with an embrace.

- *Conversational space:* Stand still and allow the international businessperson to find a comfortable speaking distance. Doing so will help establish you as a well-informed individual who deserves respect.

- *Office space:* Do not assume that international offices are arranged exactly as they are in your culture. Making assumptions about the status or importance of another person based on office arrangement can lead to uncomfortable errors in cross-cultural communication.

- *Dress and accessories:* Your physical attire and accessories send nonverbal messages: dress to convey respect for the other culture. Determine if wearing national or religious symbols on clothing or jewelry may be considered offensive by the culture with which you're interacting.

- *Time:* Beware of assuming that everyone believes in being on time—or the reverse—that being on time is unimportant. Seek to understand how the other culture views time, and then try to flex to their view. At the same time, you can help your counterpart understand and flex to your cultural view of time.

- *Silence:* Consider the differing ways that cultures use and interpret silence. Do not rush to fill the silence or be offended if others interrupt you.

- *Gender considerations:* In addition to the aspects of nonverbal communication that we have covered, an important point to remember is that men and women within cultures may differ in their use of nonverbal communication. If you'd like more information about these fascinating communication patterns and preferences, please see Deborah Tannen's book, *Talking 9 to 5*, cited in the bibliography.

CHAPTER VIII OUTLINE

CHAPTER VIII

Negotiating: Process, Persuasion, and Law

A bad compromise is better than a good lawsuit.
—VIETNAMESE PROVERB

Know each other as if you were brothers; negotiate as
if you were strangers.
—SAUDI ARABIAN PROVERB

Knowledge of cross-cultural business communication can help smooth transactions across cultural boundaries that are sometimes more formidable than physical borders. Negotiating successfully across cultures has tremendous financial implications for business. For example, U.S. exports to trading partners across the globe are nearing $600 billion even with the downturn in the worldwide economy. Knowledge of negotiating styles across cultures may influence the successful sale of a product, the formation of a joint venture, or the implementation of steps toward a merger or acquisition of another company.

Looking across borders is only a first step, however, because the very definition of negotiation differs across culture. As we discussed in Chapter 2, in low-context cultures such as the United States, negotiation usually means achieving a good outcome for both parties through a discussion of the reasons and facts involved. To someone from a high-context culture such as Mexico, negotiation has as its core element the relationship between the two parties. In such high-context cultures, facts, reasons, and pure logic are subordinate to the trust that is the necessary underpinning of any business deal. With such different definitions of negotiation, it's easy to see how cross-cultural negotiations can disappoint and frustrate both sides.

Most businesspeople understand that international negotiation is a very complex subject and that they need to pay attention to the many ways culture affects business negotiations both nationally and internationally. While negotiation across cultures is a complex subject about which volumes have been written, this chapter will briefly discuss those facets of cross-cultural negotiation that businesspeople need to consider to communicate successfully. We'll examine elements of persuasion, credibility issues, and the three major forms of law.

I. ANALYZING THE NEGOTIATION PROCESS

In the early stages of international negotiation, it's important to analyze the possible objectives and timeframe of the other party and then to select the place and players who are most likely to achieve success. Success will depend on being able to satisfy both your goals and at least some of the objectives of the other party. As the Russian proverb states, "In a deal, there are two fools, the one who asks too much and the one who asks too little." In order to prevent the all-too-often outcome of this proverb, smart negotiators will observe the following elements.

Setting objectives: Broad objectives might include your parameters for a timeframe, product specifications, and commitments for follow-up training and service. Not only will you need to set clear objectives before you enter into discussion, but you will also need to remain alert to differing cultural values that may necessitate modifying those objectives.

Selecting team members: To achieve success in your negotiations, you should devote thought and effort in choosing team members who will be knowledgeable and effective negotiators. Consider the elements of credibility when making your decision. Those elements include rank (hierarchical position), goodwill (past personal experience), expertise (knowledge), image (charisma or attractiveness), and shared values (common ground).

> Cultures in most African countries establish goodwill with the people they meet rather than with a business entity. Therefore, it's important to send team members whom you expect to be with your company for several years. In some countries, especially those where women are considered followers or second-class citizens, be sure to include male members of the negotiating team even if the team leader is a woman. Titles and rank are also more important, so include specific business titles on your business cards and include a high-ranking person to enhance credibility. Your country's embassy will be able to guide you in making contact with local businesspeople who are knowledgeable about your business or industry so that you can fine-tune the selection process.

Focusing on their needs: As you know, not every culture values the same things. The same will be true in business negotiations. For example, if you are from a culture that demands time efficiency, you may be surprised if the other players disregard your company's promise to deliver on time. If you are from a culture that expects monetary and material benefits, you may be surprised when offering the lowest price doesn't work. Understanding benefits that appeal to the needs of those with whom you are negotiating is critical to success.

> When UPS, an international package delivery service that now operates in more than 200 countries, prepared to set up locations in the former West Germany, the company offered to supply uniforms to workers as part of their contract. Unfortunately, the required brown color of the uniform shirts reminded German citizens of the "brown shirts" that are emblematic of the Nazi SA during World War II. UPS replaced the brown with a green uniform to ease the negotiating and recruiting process.

Thinking about the needs of the other party will enable you to discover the importance of relationship, trust, religion, governmental oversight, and other areas you might have overlooked if you negotiated from a culture-centric viewpoint.

Selecting a translator: Having your own translator is extremely valuable and well worth the added expense. Select a translator who has experience not only with the language, but also with the specialized vocabulary of your particular industry. It's also important to find a translator who speaks the local dialect and has a "correct" accent for maximum credibility. Your interpreter is valuable not only in translating, but also in listening in to the other team's comments. A good translator will have people skills, intelligence, and knowledge of your particular product or service.

> Russian native Janna Baiounova offered the following advice for Westerners who negotiate with Russian counterparts: "The Russian team will include at least two interpreters and members who have technical or engineering backgrounds. Your team also needs to include an excellent interpreter and well-educated technical individuals. Offer your business cards in both English and Russian, and do not make a joke or smile during the initial greeting. This is an opportunity to show that you take business seriously. It's important to provide a detailed, technical proposal in both English and Russian. Russian negotiators will tend to be direct, and there may be emotional outbursts; therefore, patience can be the Westerner's best friend. Although the process can be difficult, once you establish a personal relationship with Russian counter-parties, doing business with Russia will become fun."

Deciding on room arrangements: What is your preferred negotiating arrangement? Do you emphasize competitiveness and therefore like to "face off" with players arranged along opposite sides of a conference table? Do you emphasize collaboration and therefore prefer that players sit at a round table? Do you emphasize equality where everyone will sit along one side of a table facing a whiteboard or an audiovisual display?

Remember that physical arrangements vary even within a culture; a particular corporate culture will influence the room arrangement. For example, in the United States, formal corporate cultures may favor opposite sides of a conference table. Informal corporate cultures may favor the roundtable arrangement. Finally, some U.S. corporate cultures want to address a particular problem or objective by facing it squarely. All three arrangements can be found in various corporations within most of the world's major cultures. Clearly defining your objectives will help you determine the most suitable setting.

Considering time: As we discussed in Chapter 3, cultures define time itself differently: "relational" cultures believe that timing issues are subordinate to people issues; "transactional" cultures believe that the job comes first. For example, when negotiating the delivery of goods, knowing what the other culture considers "on time" can avoid delays and minimize frustration. If you know that a company with whom you have done business in the past is usually late with shipments, build extra time into your schedule as you negotiate. There's no sense in complaining to the party from the other culture; you will not change an entire culture's attitudes about time no matter how much you whine or badger.

Also, consider the various holidays that may affect the length of time it will take to complete a deal and the way that holidays will affect projected delivery schedules. In the United States, holidays are scattered throughout the year, but, typically, little business is conducted during the week of July 4th (Independence Day) since that is a floating holiday. Similarly, learn about holidays celebrated in the culture representing the other side of the negotiation. Your knowledge of their time issues will help you understand the constraints they face and how best to work around them.

In emails to an open conference at a multinational firm, Seita Yamaoka sought to educate co-workers about the language and customs of his native Japan. In one email, he wrote, "Have you ever heard the expression 'Golden Week?' We Japanese call the week from the end of April to the beginning of May 'Golden Week' because we have four national holidays during this week. The holidays include April 29—Green Day, May 3—Constitution Day, May 4—National Holiday, and May 5—Children's Day. If you are transacting business with Japanese companies, be careful, because most business activities stop in Japan during 'Golden Week!' "

Using patience: One of the most important negotiating tactics is patience. If you are from a low-context culture (United States, Northern Europe, Australia) seeking to negotiate with a high-context culture (Asian, Latino, African, Arab), you will have a more positive outcome if you don't expect immediate responses. In other words, not receiving an answer doesn't necessarily mean the answer is "No."

> As business director for a private university, Hyun Park was in charge of negotiating the rent of a dormitory during the 1996 Atlanta Olympic games. Although he had lived most of his life in the United States, Park used a negotiation style often employed by high-context cultures such as his native Korea.
>
> A national news organization wanted the 23-room house for three weeks and offered $30,000. Park did not respond. The news organization then offered $45,000. Park didn't respond. Totally exasperated, the U.S. news organization made its final and absolute offer of $60,000, which Park accepted.
>
> He later told a colleague, "Initially, I didn't respond because I was considering their offer, and I wasn't sure what to do about it. After they upped the offer so quickly, I waited to see what their final price might be."

Interpreting negative messages: It's crucial to understand the communication dynamics at work when low- and high-context cultures negotiate. Some high-context cultures (Asian, for example) place a value on preserving the harmony of a situation and, therefore, hesitate to say "no" explicitly. Instead of saying "no," a Japanese negotiator may state, "That may be difficult." Your interpreter will help you to understand the literal meaning of the indirect language. Even in a relatively "Westernized" country such as Russia, misunderstandings of negative messages may occur. After the "final" contract offer in a negotiation has been agreed, the Russians may request a change. No agreement is really final until the appropriate Russian representatives have signed it. The art of reading negative messages can be developed over time, and a skilled local consultant can help ensure success.

Reaching a conclusion: If you have hired an excellent interpreter, assembled a competent team, and forged a relationship over time with the other party, you will be in a good position to negotiate a positive outcome for both parties. However, the conclusion of the negotiation may not be viewed in the same way by different cultures. Just as the view of time itself is fluid in some cultures, the terms of an agreement may also remain fluid for the duration of a project. Insisting on rigid timelines and fixed contracts may be *de rigueur* in your country, but it can be counterproductive in high-context cultures. In the United States businesspeople say, "A contract is a contract." When negotiating across cultures, however, remember that issues may be revisited after the contract is signed.

Another possible barrier to concluding the negotiation is the appeal to higher authority. Whereas a U.S. negotiator may use higher authority as a ploy to delay negotiations, other cultures may actually have to obtain approval from governmental sources or senior members of their organizational hierarchy. Ask your consultant about governmental approval at the outset of your negotiations. Build in extra time for approval through channels after the conclusion of your negotiations.

Planning for concessions: Parties to a negotiation usually begin from vastly different starting points; some favor extreme positions while others favor more moderate opening arguments. The use of concessions differs, with some cultures allowing immediate and repeated concessions and others viewing them as a sign of weakness to be avoided.

For example, Israeli negotiators have a reputation for steadfastness and see concessions as a painful sacrifice, a form of failure. Conversely, in China, a successful negotiation will arrive at consensus that saves face for every member of the negotiating team. The following illustrates some of the knowledge that Western negotiators should consider when meeting their counterparts from an Eastern country such as China.

In keeping with a preference for linear, logical thinking, a Western negotiation team will typically first decide its best-case position, then determine its bottom "walkaway" position, and then structure a set of concessions that lies in between the two extremes. This approach is dangerous in China, particularly when applied to price negotiations. When a Western team makes its first concession, say by moving from $10 to $8 per unit, it sends a signal that the first price is meaningless and that there is a lot of negotiating room left. As extremely price-sensitive negotiators, the Chinese will apply tremendous pressure for more concessions.

A better approach is to offer a price with room for a token concession at the end of negotiations and then offer concessions of a different kind, such as training or after-sales service, instead of additional "slices" off the price. This emphasizes the overall value of the offering and steers the discussion away from price alone.

Negotiating in China, Meridian Resources,
Global Skills Update

II. ENHANCING YOUR PERSUASIVENESS

In addition to thinking through the negotiation process, think about how you can enhance your persuasiveness. In *Guide to Managerial Communication,* Mary Munter covers the logic of the message, the emotions of the audience, and the credibility of the speaker. We'll examine how culture affects these elements.

Logic of message: The type of reasoning used in logical arguments can differ widely across cultures. Some cultures prefer inductive, indirect reasoning that looks first at examples and then forms a generalization. For example, the French tend to prefer inductive reasoning and relish a well-built argument. Other cultures prefer deductive, direct reasoning that begins with a generalization and then looks at examples to prove it. Corporations in the United States tend to prefer deductive reasoning. They want the "bottom line" first and then the explanations.

Using the wrong form of logic can impede the progress of your negotiation. Looking at logic preferences of the other culture early in the game will help guide you to construct effective presentations and written materials for your negotiation. If you are from a culture that favors direct, deductive reasoning, you will be most effective if you allow time for indirect arguments to unfold.

Emotions of audience: How does your audience feel about your message? If they are feeling anxious, fearful, or jealous, then your persuasiveness will depend on overcoming objections by (1) encouraging them to understand that there is a problem and offering a solution, (2) enumerating the points of agreement to encourage buy-in, (3) putting your proposal in the simplest form—perhaps offering a pilot program first, and (4) surfacing possible objections and addressing them. If they are feeling pride, excitement, or hope, your communication task will be easier. If they are disinterested, your first task will be to arouse their interest by emphasizing benefits based on the cultural values we have discussed.

Knowing how the culture expresses emotion is also important in intercultural communication. For example, most South American and Arab cultures believe that an open show of emotion indicates your interest, concern, commitment, and passion. But Northern European cultures don't trust emotion and will assume that an overt display of emotion is unprofessional or manipulative. Understanding how cultures use emotion and flexing to their emotional style is an important element of cross-cultural persuasion.

Another influence on the audience's emotions has to do with the setting and room arrangement.

Credibility of speaker: Munter lists five factors that are the most important in establishing credibility: rank, goodwill, expertise, image, and common ground. All five of these elements can influence the outcome of a negotiation.

- *Rank:* Munter defines rank as hierarchical power. Rank is especially important in cultures that clearly define the hierarchy of leaders and followers (described in Chapter 4). Even if someone represents status in the hierarchy, they may lack the family connections or educational affiliation to achieve credibility. In cultures where the power is more flat or democratic, rank will be relatively less important. Middle managers are trusted to effectively negotiate with upper-level managers of the other party, and family and university affiliations are much less important.

   Munter points out that people without high rank can enhance their credibility by associating themselves with or citing a high-ranking person. In some cultures, for example, you might ask a high-ranking person to make introductions. Or you might use a letter of introduction or a teleconference if the higher-ranking person cannot attend the negotiation.

- *Goodwill:* Goodwill is the personal relationship or personal history with the other party. The importance of goodwill varies from culture to culture. For example, forming solid relationships over time will be crucial in negotiations with high-context cultures (discussed in Chapter 2). However, the following scenario is typical of the differing way that many low-context cultures, such as the United States, view goodwill.

   "I'm not sure about this contract offer," Jim reported to his colleague David at Redstone Research in Santa Barbara. "I don't think they really care what happens to our business."

   "Look, the software works great. We've tested it, they offered it at a good price, and they provide training. Nothing else matters," replied David.

   In such low-context cultures emphasizing material benefits may be the key to establishing goodwill credibility.

- *Expertise:* Munter explains expertise as "knowledge and competence." The extent to which expertise matters, however, is influenced by culture. Low-context cultures may value expertise over the relationship; a businessperson will need to clearly establish past experience with successful projects and sound technical knowledge to be thought credible. Although expertise is important in high-context cultures, it is secondary to relationships, and it will, therefore, be demonstrated to an audience in ways that preserve relationships.

Dr. Emmett Smith, a consultant in international negotiations, observed, "To say 'We have the best engineers and the most advanced design' might play well in Germany. In Japan, however, it would seem rude. The Japanese would say, 'We have some small knowledge of this issue.' " Similarly to other high-context cultures, their expertise would be stated indirectly and respectfully.

- *Image:* According to Munter, image involves attractiveness—the extent to which the other party admires you. If you look and sound attractive to your audience, you will automatically have the advantage of image credibility. In some cultures, men are preferred over women, age is preferred over youth, and people tend to identify with someone from their own ethnicity. Although we cannot change our gender, age, or ethnicity, successful negotiators recognize that the greater the differences in image between the parties, the harder they will have to work to establish credibility. In cases where the differences are large, additional care to the other credibility factors can help overcome doubts based on factors that cannot be altered.

Anita Barton uses her MBA and an MPH (Masters of Public Health) to consult with corporations in formulating their drug and alcohol abuse policies and treatment programs. Because she is an attractive blonde in her early 30's, she sometimes finds it difficult to establish image credibility with potential business clients. Therefore, Anita is careful to spend time discussing her experience and trying to find common ground through education, work with client organizations, and other evidence of her credibility. Her business has thrived in spite of the "handicaps" of age, gender, and physical appearance.

- *Common ground:* Common ground involves values, ideas, problems, or needs that are shared by both parties. Examples of shared tangible values include profit, savings, bonuses, or product discounts. Career or task benefits include solving problems, saving time, or advancing prestige. Ego benefits can include self-worth, accomplishment, and achievement. Group benefits can include relationship enhancement, group identity, solidarity, or consensus. Since not every culture values the same things, the goal of effective intercultural communication is to discover similar values.

At a conference on international banking held in Chicago, a consultant in cross-cultural communication asked the multinational executives to list and rank-order their values. Lists included family, prestige, profit, security, love, power, religion, assertiveness, and patience, among others. When asked to select their number-one value, the executives were surprised to find that the highest ranked value differed widely among the diverse cultures represented by the executives. In fact, values that some participants thought were fundamental didn't even appear on other participants' lists. For example, a Lebanese American reported that there was no exact word for "privacy" in Arabic; the closest translation was "loneliness." The executives learned that an important step in successful cross-cultural negotiations is to explore the other culture and uncover values that might be shared.

To establish credibility in any negotiation, it's important to assess the values of your team and the other team, especially if you represent different cultures. If you take the time to discover what you and the other team have in common, you can emphasize shared values and strengthen your credibility.

Although you need to understand persuasion for any negotiation, when you're negotiating across cultures, you'll also need to pay attention to international law and the rules of trade. The following section will provide a brief overview of the three major forms of law.

III. UNDERSTANDING INTERNATIONAL LAW

Legal systems consist of enforceable rules that govern relationships among individuals within the context of the greater society. Law, however, is indisputably influenced by culture, as underscored in the Slovak proverb, "Custom and law are sisters." Unfortunately, many businesspeople tend to be ethnocentric and culture-centric in their understanding of legal systems.

> A former chief negotiator for the U.S. Attorney General stated at his retirement, "Twenty years ago, I did antitrust work for clients like General Motors, and at that time I could do that and know nothing but American antitrust law. We have been sitting on our own continent, not having to know much about legal practice in other parts of the world. Now, that has totally changed—totally."

The following section explains three forms of law that can influence the outcome of any international negotiation: Common Law, Code Law, and Sharia Law. Other forms of law may be based on local custom (such as tribal law). It's essential to your business interests to obtain the advice of a local legal representative early in your negotiation.

Common law: The overall goal of common law is to make decisions consistent with previous rulings or precedents. The common law system originated with the Norman invasion of England in 1066, when William the Conqueror established the king's courts to bring together the many local systems of law in his territory. The common practices of these courts became the source of law used today. Some of the countries that use common law include Australia, Bangladesh, Canada, Ghana, India, Israel, Jamaica, Kenya, Malaysia, New Zealand, Nigeria, Singapore, United Kingdom, the United States (with the exception of the state of Louisiana), and Zambia.

Because common law varied from state to state in the early history of the U.S., it was difficult to conduct business across states with any assurance of redress for problems. To address these concerns, the Uniform Commercial Code (UCC) established in 1952 governs commercial law in all fifty states, the District of Columbia, and the Virgin Islands.

Code law: In contrast to common law, which is based on past precedents, code law establishes rules to be followed and enforced in the future. Important historical examples of code law include the Code of Hammurabi (in ancient Babylon), Roman law, and Napoleonic law. Countries that use code law include Argentina, Austria, Brazil, Chile, China, Egypt, Finland, France, Germany, Greece, Indonesia, Iran, Italy, Japan, Mexico, Poland, South Africa, South Korea, Sweden, Tunisia, and Venezuela. One state in the U.S., Louisiana, follows code law because of its unique ties to France.

Unlike common law, code law doesn't rely on precedence for its interpretation. Although code law may be influenced by earlier court decisions, these precedents are not as binding as in common law. In addition, decisions are made by judges rather than by a jury of peers in nations that follow code law.

Sharia law: In Muslim countries, Sharia law governs every facet of life, both public and private. For example, by law, alcohol is forbidden and, in some countries, the rights of women are limited. However, adherence to Sharia law varies from country to country, and often Muslims who travel abroad are not as strictly bound to their legal code as they would be in their home country. Be aware, however, that before you travel to a traditional Muslim country, you should inquire about proper attire and behavior such as restrictions regarding alcohol. Most state departments provide information about such aspects of traveling to a foreign country. (For example, see www.state.gov/countries.)

Sharia law is based on the teachings of the Islamic holy book, the Koran. The keystone of Sharia law is ethical behavior. One of the most noted features of Sharia is the fact that it forbids the collection of interest. In addition, those who do business together are expected to share risks and gambling is strictly forbidden. The following scenario illustrates some of these features of Sharia law.

> "Could you please explain how you lend money without collecting interest?" John asked Hussein, who was arranging a banking deal from Riyad.
>
> "We practice a form of leasing called *ijara*. We purchase the equipment that a business needs and then lease it back to them."
>
> "So the business never owns the equipment?"
>
> "Well, there are actually several types of lease arrangements. One that we use is called *ijara wa iqtina* or lease purchase. In that situation, the business purchases the equipment from the bank at the end of the lease. We usually apply the rental payments to the purchase price."

"Isn't the bank assuming more of the risk?"

"Yes," Hussein answered. "However, our leases are asset-backed and we can sublease them. We also periodically adjust our rental rates similar to your floating interest rates in the U.S. Our method of banking helps us form a partnership with our customer."

David Wohabe, Wohabe Law Offices,
New York

When Muslim families wish to own homes in the U.S., the private lender, Freddie Mac, offers a way around the interest dilemma in an unusual blending of cultures. Freddie Mac, a company that does not provide loans to consumers, buys Islamic housing contracts from American Finance House-Lariba. The Muslim homebuyer signs an agreement with American Finance House-Lariba that stipulates maximum monthly payment based on the selling price of the house and the rental value. Freddie Mac then purchases these contracts. Fair lending law in the U.S. ensures that even non-Muslims can apply for this type of loan if they wish to do so.

International rules: Although negotiating and conducting business with another country carry risks, organizations have developed to facilitate international and regional business. Some of these organizations include the World Trade Organization (WTO), the European Union (EU), and the North American Free Trade Agreement (NAFTA).

- *The World Trade Organization (WTO)* evolved from the General Agreement on Tariffs and Trade (GATT) and was established in 1994 under an agreement signed by representatives from over a hundred nations. Under the WTO, the concept of "most-favored nation status" was developed where members accord each other favorable treatment in tariff reduction, investment policies, and dispute resolution.

- *The European Union (EU)* currently comprises twenty-seven member states: Austria, Belgium, Bulgaria, Cyprus, the Czech Republic, Denmark, Estonia, Finland, France, Germany, Greece, Hungary, Ireland, Italy, Latvia, Lithuania, Luxembourg, Malta, the Netherlands, Poland, Portugal, Romania, Slovakia, Slovenia, Spain, Sweden, and the United Kingdom. The purpose of the EU is to promote trade among member nations. A representative Council of Ministers coordinates economic policies that are administered by the EU's own Court of Justice. EU directives govern issues such as environmental law, product liability, anticompetitive practices, and laws governing corporations.

- *The North American Free Trade Agreement (NAFTA)* eliminates tariffs among the U.S., Canada, and Mexico, thus providing a competitive advantage. Unlike some other trade agreements, NAFTA applies to services as well as goods. Therefore, U.S. financial institutions that once needed an office in Mexico or Canada will be able to offer financial services from their U.S. location.

- *Mediation and arbitration* may become necessary when disputes arise. When rules are broken, arbitration is a less costly option than litigation: as the German proverb advises, "A lean agreement is better than a fat lawsuit." Some of the organizations that offer assistance with mediation and arbitration include the International Chamber of Commerce, the United Nations Foreign Arbitral Awards, and the international division of the American Arbitration Association.

Internet resources: Many websites exist to provide information on international trade law. A web search using the key words "international business" will provide information on the laws of each country and regulations governing international trade and will help you find an internationally trained or bilingual attorney. Helpful sites include the following:

- The United Nations provides an excellent resource for cultural information and law at www.un.org.

- The European Union website offers a treasure trove of information regarding standards in products, goods, services, and intellectual property as well as information on legal standards for member nations at www.un.org.

- U.S. Free Trade Agreements website can help companies who wish to enter and compete in the global marketplace at www.export.gov/fta.

IV. GUIDELINES FOR NEGOTIATION

Do your homework! Search websites for specific information on each country. Be alert to magazine and news articles that contain background information on international businesses and the difficulties they may have faced in negotiating across cultures. Talk to others who have conducted business with the culture you are targeting. Also, consider these guidelines:

- *Contract a skilled local consultant* to guide your negotiations.
- *Set realistic objectives* for your negotiation.
- *Consider the negotiation* from the other culture's point of view. What will *they* want?
- *Select team members* who have credibility and knowledge of cross-cultural issues.
- *Design realistic timeframes* for delivery or implementation.
- *Find a translator* who understands your objectives.
- *Decide on room arrangements* and analyze the setting.
- *Allow time* to develop relationships with those from other cultures.
- *Learn* as much as possible about the legal system of the other party.
- *Obtain help* from an attorney familiar with both legal systems.
- *Specify arbitration over litigation* in your contracts in the case of disputes and *determine* where litigation will be conducted if the need arises—your courts or theirs?

Conclusion

Learning is like rowing upstream; not to advance is to drop back.

—CHINESE PROVERB

In his acceptance speech for the Nobel Peace Prize, Jimmy Carter said, "The greater ease of travel and communication has not been matched by equal understanding and mutual respect." Our hope is that this book will increase "understanding and mutual respect" across cultures and help to counteract Carter's assertion.

Our book was written to provide essential information and practical examples about important aspects of intercultural communication in a brief, reader-friendly format. In writing this book, we strove to:

- **Increase your knowledge about cultural groups** with which you live, work, and conduct business: Diverse cultures have come up with a dazzling variety of ways to look at existence; sharing this legacy of diverse cultures enriches your ability to think, to cope, and to solve problems. Acquiring cultural knowledge will provide insight into your business colleagues and clients.

- **Encourage you to examine your own personal communication patterns** and assess their effectiveness in initiating and developing successful business relationships with people from diverse cultures. Learning about other cultures and developing cultural understanding allows you to access a greater range of personal problem-solving tools and coping skills. It allows you to become a citizen of the world, more global in your outlook and behavior, and, therefore, more effective personally and professionally.

- **Help you develop creative responses** and "flexing" skills in problematic intercultural situations by providing thoughtful and practical skills and examples.

In addition to the guidelines we offer at the end of each chapter to help you communicate with sensitivity, we'd like to end our book with two over-arching recommendations:

- *Continue learning:* We urge you to consider this book as the first step in a lifelong commitment to competence in cross-cultural communication. The quest to learn about world cultures will take you on a lifelong, but fascinating and worthwhile, journey. Continue to read, observe, and learn as much as possible. To this end, we provide a list of suggested books and films to help you on your journey.

  As a human being, you are part of the immeasurably rich heritage of world cultures. The knowledge you will gain from considering the assumptions, perspectives, and solutions provided by other cultures will broaden your horizons, enhancing both your personal growth and your resourcefulness in today's multicultural business environment.

- *Develop relationships:* Devote the necessary time to get to know people from other cultures. Eat with them, drink with them, get to know their families, and invite them to know yours. Spending time with your intercultural business partners will prove your commitment to the relationship.

  Forging personal relationships with people from other cultures will allow you to acquire first-hand knowledge about cultural variety, complexity, and change. It will enhance your ability to be a front-line player in developing cultural synergy. It will allow you to participate in the global understanding and cooperation that have become essential for personal survival, professional success, national harmony, and international understanding.

The chart on the next page should be interpreted as a broad-brush, simplified listing of general characteristics and tendencies, not as a definitive series of factual statements about cultures. We are fully aware of the differences that exist among individuals, even within a single-language community. We nonetheless think that it will help you chart your journey.

CROSS-CULTURAL COMMUNICATION SUMMARY CHART	
North America, North & West Europe, Australia, New Zealand	**Mediterranean countries, Asia, Africa, Middle East, Central and South America**
Individual	Collective
Transactional	Relational
Competitive	Collaborative
Direct	Indirect
Monochronic time	Polychronic time
Emphasis on content	Emphasis on context
Linear logic	Circular reasoning
Flat organization	Hierarchical structure
Trust in words	Trust in silence
Reliance on litigation	Reliance on mediation

Cultural Questionnaire: A Tool for Understanding Your Culture

The following questionnaire is designed to help you understand your own cultural tendencies. Select the answer that most closely approximates your beliefs and behavior. For maximum growth, we recommend that you answer the questionnaire before you read the book and then review your answers after you've finished reading.

Chapter I. Relationships: Individual or Collective?

1. Your group has been assigned a new project. What is your feeling about it?

    (A) You would just as soon do it on your own and finish faster.
    (B) You look forward to learning more by working with the team.

2. The division in your company that has the most sales for the third quarter will win a 10 percent bonus. There is an additional 10 percent bonus for the person with highest sales in the overall company. How would you approach the contest?

    (A) Double your efforts to win the 10 percent individual bonus.
    (B) Meet with your group to devise a plan to ensure that your division wins.

3. You are taking a train or entering a restaurant. Neither the train car nor the restaurant is full. Which of the following options would you choose?

    (A) You select a seat away from other people.
    (B) You select a seat near other people.

4. Your company is expanding to South America, and you have been sent to meet with the Venezuelan representative. How do you approach the meeting?

(A) You fly to Caracas, plan to meet, and return the following day.

(B) You fly to Caracas a day early to tour so that you can comment on the beauty of the countryside and the history of the nation when you meet with the representative.

5. Your meetings with the international team have lasted all day. What do you do after hours?

(A) Make your excuses and retire for the night.

(B) Believe it is your obligation to go out with the group no matter how tired you are.

Calculate your score. If you answered with more As, you probably come from an individualistic culture. More Bs may indicate that you come from a collective culture.

Chapter II. Social Framework: High Context or Low Context?

6. You usually pick up the body language of others and know intuitively if something is bothering them.

(A) No

(B) Yes

7. Your colleague says, "This department has never lost so much money." How do you feel about the comment?

(A) The comment annoys you because you know that several years ago the department had a loss that was a quarter-of-a-million more than the present problem.

(B) You understand that your colleague didn't mean what he said literally; rather, he was commenting on the difficulties the company has been facing.

8. The new department head hands down a list of rules for employees. You react as follows:

(A) You tack up the rules in your cubicle so that you can refer to them periodically.

(B) You glance at the rules and plan to follow them or bend them depending on the situation.

9. Your manager has given her analysis of the department's losses in the first quarter. You disagree with the manager's assessment.

   (A) You openly state your disagreement.

   (B) You cross your arms, lean back, and wait to be asked your opinion.

10. When deciding on a person to promote in your department, you face the problem of choosing between two equally qualified individuals, one of whom is your cousin. What do you do?

   (A) Choose the applicant who is not your cousin.

   (B) Choose your cousin.

Calculate your score. If you answered with more As, you probably come from a low-context culture. More Bs may indicate that you come from a high-context culture.

Chapter III. Time: Linear, Flexible, or Cyclical?

11. You are on vacation. The mass transit train arrives late, and the platform is quite crowded. What do you do?

   (A) Push forward.

   (B) Wait patiently to board.

12. At the office, you are on the phone when you see a colleague walk toward you. Because he's been traveling, you haven't seen him in a month. What do you do?

   (A) Smile and wave and hold up your finger to indicate, "Wait a minute."

   (B) Terminate the call so you can greet your colleague.

13. Do you carry a PDA, day planner, or calendar with appointments?

   (A) Yes

   (B) No

14. Are you comfortable doing multiple tasks at the same time?

   (A) No

   (B) Yes

15. Are your business colleagues and the group you socialize with usually similar?

   (A) No

   (B) Yes

Calculate your score. If you answered with more As, you may tend toward a linear-time orientation. If you scored more Bs, you may be from a flexible- or cyclical-time orientation.

Chapter IV. Power: Hierarchical or Democratic?

16. You've worked with the new vice president for several months and have formed an opinion of her. You like her for the following reason.

    (A) She listens to various opinions and seeks consensus.

    (B) She takes charge and doesn't put up with any nonsense.

17. You have been selected by the head of your department to be a team member on a big project. At the first team meeting, some people suggest that the team select a leader.

    (A) You disagree. No one should be singled out as higher in rank than the others.

    (B) You agree. The team will accomplish more with clear leadership and structure.

18. Your division is facing cutbacks, and you must decide how this should be accomplished. What would you do?

    (A) Call a meeting of employees to discuss options.

    (B) Cut everyone's salary by 3%.

19. You've been introduced to an economist from a prominent university in Madrid. You address him in the following manner:

    (A) It's nice to meet you, Rodrigo.

    (B) It's good to meet you, Dr. Barbato.

20. You will be meeting with representatives of a South Korean electronics firm. You decide to wear the following:

    (A) Business casual attire.

    (B) Business attire.

Calculate your score. If you answered with more As, you may tend toward a more democratic view of organizational culture. If you scored more Bs, you probably have a more hierarchical view of organizational culture.

Bibliography

Adler, N., *International Dimensions of Organizational Behavior,* 5th ed., Cincinnati, Ohio: South-Western, 2008.

Anderson, J.W., "A Comparison of Arab and American Perceptions of Effective Persuasion," *Intercultural Communication: A Reader,* Belmont, California: Wadsworth, 1997, 98–106.

Beamer, L. and I. Varner, *Intercultural Communication in the Global Marketplace,* 4th ed., Boston, Massachusetts: McGraw-Hill Irwin, 2008.

Chaney, L. and J. Martin, *Intercultural Business Communication,* 4th ed., Upper Saddle River, New Jersey: Prentice Hall, 2007.

De Ley, G., *International Dictionary of Proverbs,* New York: Hippocrene Books, 1998.

Ferraro, G., *The Cultural Dimension of International Business,* 6th ed., Upper Saddle River, New Jersey: Prentice Hall, 2010.

Greenberg, E. and K. Weber, *Generation We,* Emeryville, CA: Pachatusan Publishing, 2008.

Gudykunst, W. and T. Nishida, *Bridging Japanese/North American Differences,* Thousand Oaks, California: Sage Publications, 1994.

Hall, E. and M. Hall, *Understanding Cultural Differences,* Yarmouth, Maine: Intercultural Press, 1990.

Hofstede, G., "Motivation, Leadership, and Organization: Do American Theories Apply Abroad?" *Organizational Dynamics* (Summer 1980).

_____ "The Confucius Connection: From Cultural Roots to Economic Growth," Organizational Dynamics (Spring 1988).

Jentz, G., R. Miller, and F. Cross, *West's Business Law*, Alt. Ed., Cincinnati, Ohio: Thomson Learning, 2007.

Kenton, S.B. and D. Valentine, *CrossTalk: Communicating in a Multicultural Workplace*, Upper Saddle River, New Jersey: Prentice Hall, 1997.

Kohls, R. *Survival Kit for Overseas Living*, 4th ed., Yarmouth, Maine: Intercultural Press, Inc., 2001.

Lewis, R. D., *When Cultures Collide*, London, England: Nicholas Brealey Publishing, 1999.

Moran, R., P. Harris, and S. Moran, *Managing Cultural Differences*, 7th ed., Houston, Texas: Gulf Publishing, 2007.

Moran, R. and W. Stripp, *Successful International Business Negotiations*, Houston, Texas: Gulf Publishing, 1991.

Morrison, T., W. Conaway, and G. Borden, *Kiss, Bow, or Shake Hands: How to do Business in Sixty Countries*, Holbrook, Massachusetts: Bob Adams, 1994.

Munter, M., "Cross-Cultural Communication for Managers," *Business Horizons* (May-June, 1993), 69–76.

_____ *Guide to Managerial Communication*, 8th ed., Upper Saddle River, New Jersey: Prentice Hall, 2010.

Neuliep, J. W., *Intercultural Communication: A Contextual Approach*, New York: Houghton Mifflin, 2000.

Nydell, M. K., *Understanding Arabs: A Guide for Westerners*, Yarmouth, Maine: Intercultural Press, 1987.

Reid, T. R., *Confucius Lives Next Door: What Living in the East Teaches Us About Living in the West*, New York: Random House, 1999.

Ribbink, K., "Seven Ways to Better Communicate in Today's Diverse Workplace," *Harvard Management Communication Letter* (November 2002), 6–8.

Rosensweig, J., *Winning the Global Game*, New York: The Free Press, 1998.

Said, E., *Orientalism,* New York: Random House, 1978.

Samovar, L., R. Porter, and L. Stefani, *Communication Between Cultures,* 6th ed., Belmont, California: Wadsworth Publishing, 2006.

Sokuvitz, S., "Global Business Communication," *Business Communication Quarterly* (March 2002), 56–69.

Tapscott, D., *Grown Up Digital,* New York: McGraw Hill, 2009.

Ting-Toomey, S., *Communicating Across Cultures,* New York: The Guilford Press, 1999.

Victor, D., *International Business Communication,* New York: Harper Collins, 2002.

Westin, A. F., *Privacy and Freedom,* Chicago, Illinois: Atheneum, 1967.

Yip, G., *Total Global Strategy II,* Upper Saddle River, New Jersey: Prentice Hall, 2003.

Suggested Readings: Novels to Explore Culture

Because literature can reveal culture, the following novels can be useful when learning about intercultural communication.

Far East

James Clavell, *Tai-Pan* and *Noble House* (Hong Kong & China), *Shōgun* (Japan)
Denise Chong, *The Concubine's Children* (China)
Austin Coates, *Myself A Mandarin* (Hong Kong & China)
Anne Fadiman, *The Spirit Catches You And You Fall Down* (the Hmong)
Frances Fitzgerald, *Fire in the Lake* (Vietnam)
Howard Golden, *Memoirs of a Geisha* (Japan)
Bette Bao Lord, *Spring Moon* (China)
Fae Myenne Ng, *Bone* (China)
Mei Ng, *Eating Chinese Food Naked* (China)
Chang-Rae Lee, *Native Speaker* (Korea)
Mark Salzman, *Iron and Silk* (China)
Lisa See, *Snow Flower and the Secret Fan* (China)
Julie Shigekuni, *A Bridge Between Us* (Japan)
Amy Tan, any of her novels, especially *The Kitchen God's Wife* (China)
Mia Yun, *House of the Winds* (Korea)

Middle East

James Clavell, *Whirlwind* (Iran)
Louis de Bernières, *Birds Without Wings* (Turkey)
Lawrence Durrell, *The Alexandria Quartet* (Egypt)

William Forbis, *The Fall of the Peacock Throne* (Iran)
Naguib Mahfouz, *Palace Walk, Palace of Desire,* and *Sugar Street*
(Egypt)
Edward Said, *Out of Place*
Ahdaf Soueif, *The Map of Love* (Palestine)

India

Mulk Raj Anand, *The Untouchable*
Shauna Singh Baldwin, *What the Body Remembers*
Jhumpa Lahiri, Interpreter of Maladies and Unaccustomed Earth
Kamala Markandaya, *Nectar in a Sieve*
Rohinton Mistry, *A Fine Balance*
Bharati Mukherjee, *Desirable Daughters*
Arundhati Roy, *The God of Small Things*
Salman Rushdie, *Midnight's Children*
Paul Scott, The Raj Quartet, Staying On, and The Alien Sky
Vikram Seth, *A Suitable Boy*
Bapsi Sidhwa, *Cracking India* and *An American Brat*

Hispanic, Latino, and Caribbean cultures

Isabelle Allende, any of her novels (Latin America)
Julia Alvarez, *How the Garcia Girls Lost Their Accents* (Hispanic
and Latino)
Edwige Danticat, *Breath, Eyes, Memory* and *Krik? Krak!* (Haiti)
Cristina Garcia, *Dreaming in Cuban* (Cuba)
Oscar Hijuelos, *Empress of the Splendid Season* (Cuba)
Jamaica Kincaid, any of her novels (Jamaica & the Caribbean)
Nicholasa Mohr, *Nilda* (Puerto Rico)
*V.S. Naipaul, The Middle Passage, Among the Believers: An Islamic
Journey, and A Flag on the Island* (West Indies & South America)
Jean Rhys, *Wide Sargasso Sea*
Any of the works of Alarcón, Borges, Cervantes, Lorca

Russia

Anton Chekhov, any of his plays
Fyodor Dostoevsky, any of his novels, especially *The Brothers
Karamazov*
Vladimir Nabokov, any of his novels
Hedrick Smith, *The Russians*

Victor Pelevin, Omon Ra, Buddha's Little Finger, and Generation OEP
Alexander Solzhenitsyn, any of his novels
Leo Tolstoy, any of his novels
Mikhail Zoshchenko, *Scenes from the Bathhouse*

Europe and the U.S.

Austen, Bennett, the Brontë sisters, Chaucer, Conrad, Delderfield,
    Dickens, Eliot, Fellowes, Fielding, Galsworthy, Larkin, Lear,
    Lessing, Maugham, McEwan, O'Faolin, Orwell, Shakespeare,
    Shaw, Sterne, Swift, Thackeray, Trollope, Waugh, Wilde,
    Wodehouse (England and the U.K.)
Baldwin, Capote, Chernow, Crane, Defoe, Dreiser, Emerson,
    Faulkner, Fitzgerald, Hawthorne, Hemingway, Hughes, Hurston,
    James, Kerouac, London, Melville, Miller, T. Morrison, Oates,
    O'Connor, Parker, Roth, Steinbeck, Twain, Updike, Williams,
    T. Wolfe, Wright (U.S.)
Balzac, Camus, Colette, de Beauvoir, Diderot, Dumas, Feydeau,
    Flaubert, Gide, Malraux, Molière, Montaigne, Proust, Rabelais,
    Sartre, Simenon, Voltaire, Zola (France)
Brecht, Goethe, Grass, Kafka, Rilke (Germany)
Dinesen, Ibsen, Strindberg (the Scandinavian countries)

Suggested Films: Movies to Explore Culture

The cinema is a powerful medium to reveal culture. The films listed below can provide a useful tool for helping you learn about intercultural communication.

Africa

Beat the Drum, God Grew Tired of Us, The Gods Must Be Crazy, Massai, Ramparts of Clay, Tsotsi, A World Apart.

China

The Blue Kite, Crouching Tiger Hidden Dragon, Eat Drink Man Woman, Farewell My Concubine, Ju Dou, The King of Masks, Not One Less, Raise the Red Lantern, Red Sorghum, Shower, Up the Yangtze, The Wedding Banquet, Yi Yi.

Europe

Amélie, Billy Elliot, The Best of Youth, The Bicycle Thief, Cabaret, Chariots of Fire, Children of Paradise, A Fish Called Wanda, 42 Up, The 400 Blows, Grand Illusion, 84 Charing Cross Road, An Ideal Husband, The Leopard, My Life as a Dog, The Lives of Others, Pelle the Conqueror, Umberto D.

India

Bend it like Beckham, Bhaji on the Beach, Delhi-6, Distant Thunder, Earth, Fire, Gandhi, The Home and the World, Mahanagar, Mississippi Masala, Monsoon Wedding, Salaam Bombay!, Slumdog Millionaire, Veer-Zaara, Water, The World of Apu.

Japan

Dreams, Early Summer, The Family Game, Fear and Trembling, The Funeral, Ikuru, Late Spring, Life of Oharu, Lost in Translation, Nobody Knows, Seven Samurai, Shall We Dance?, Still Walking, Tokyo Story.

Latin America

Amores Perros, Bye Bye Brazil, Central Station, City of God, El Norte, El Super, Family Law, Far Away and Long Ago, Il Postino, Kiss of the Spider Woman, Like Water for Chocolate, Missing, The Motorcycle Diaries, The Official Story, The Spirit of the Beehive.

Middle East

The Band's Visit, Caramel, Children of Heaven, Color of Paradise, Kandahar, Lawrence of Arabia, Le Grand Voyage, Life, and Nothing More, Offside, Osama, Yol, Offside, Paradise Now, Persepolis, The Syrian Bride, A Time for Drunken Horses, Ushpizin, Waltz with Bashir.

Russia and Eastern Europe

Alexandra, Andrei Rublev, Anna, Ballad of a Soldier, Burnt by the Sun, Closely Watched Trains, The Decalogue, Divided We Fall, Doctor Zhivago, The Firemen's Ball, 4 Months, 3 Weeks and 2 Days, Kolya, Little Vera, Loves of a Blonde, Mother and Son, Moscow Does Not Believe in Tears, The Shop on Main Street, Siberiade.

South East Asia, Australia, New Zealand

The Betrayal, Cyclo, Indochine, Journey From the Fall, The Killing Fields, The Quiet American, Rabbit-Proof Fence, The Way Home, Whale Rider.

United States

All the President's Men, American Graffiti, Apocalypse Now, Citizen Kane, 42nd Street, The Deer Hunter, Giant, The Godfather series, The Man Who Came to Dinner, M*A*S*H, O Brother, Where Art Thou?, Mr. Smith Goes to Washington, Saving Private Ryan, 1776, Show Boat, To Kill a Mockingbird, 12 Angry Men, You Can't Take it with You.

Index